RED PANDA

UNICORN WRITING MAGIC

THE ULTIMATE LEARN-TO-WRITE PRACTICE BOOK

RED PANDA

Published by Red Panda, an imprint of Westland Books, a division of Nasadiya Technologies Private Limited, in 2025

No. 269/2B, First Floor, 'Irai Arul', Vimalraj Street, Nethaji Nagar, Alapakkam Main Road, Maduravoyal, Chennai 600095

ISBN 9789360452674

10 9 8 7 6 5 4 3 2 1

Book design by Mukul Chand

Images sourced from Shutterstock

Printed at Saurabh Printers Pvt. Ltd

Contents

Sparkle and Scribble

Join us on a magical handwriting journey! This unicorn-themed handwriting workbook is meant to make learning enjoyable, exciting and rewarding for your little ones as they enter the world of writing. Here are some sparkling tips to enable them to make the most out of it:

First Things First: Holding the Pencil Right

Before going on to the activities, make sure your child grips the pencil (not a pen) just right—like a magic wand about to create magic! A proper grip (known as the tripod grip uses thumb, index and middle fingers) allows them greater control and less strain. You may even consider using silicone pencil grips to help get them underway.

Step-by-Step Learning

This book is divided into four sections, each honing your kid's fundamental skills:

1. **Pencil Control:** In the first section, drawing lines, curves and shapes will provide the ground for good handwriting skills. Ask your child to trace the patterns and build consistent hand movements.
2. **Numbers and Alphabets:** In the second half your child will move on to forming numbers and letters.
3. **Writing Words:** Basic word exercises consolidate fluency and enhance confidence in writing and reading.
4. **Motor Skills Boosters:** Enjoyable activities such as colouring, doodling, making dough balls and finger exercises enhance hand strength and coordination.

Practice Made Fun!

- **10 Minutes-a-Day:** Writing practice is best in short bursts. Encourage your child to dedicate 10 minutes daily to enhance your writing skills and stay enthusiastic.
- **Use the Stickers!** Reward small triumphs with the provided magical unicorn stickers to maximise motivation.
- **Praise and Encourage:** Learning involves mistakes! Celebrate progress, not perfection. For any tricky formations, have your child trace it in the air or paper with their finger. Then try again with a pencil.

A Journey of Confidence and Joy

This book is a handwriting system that instills confidence, patience and a love for learning.
Each line, number, or letter has a starting dot. Guide your child to follow the arrow to complete it correctly.

With your help, each page finished will be one step closer to becoming a master of writing.
Let's make this a fun experience—10 minutes a day!

Happy Writing!

The Mighty Standing Line

Trace the pink lines with your finger.
Then use a pencil to trace the practice lines.
Begin at the dot, follow the arrows and stay on the dotted path.

Lines

The Laid-Back Sleeping Line

Trace the dotted pink lines with your finger.

Use a pencil to trace the dotted practice lines.

Start →

Start →

Start →

Start →

Start →

Start →

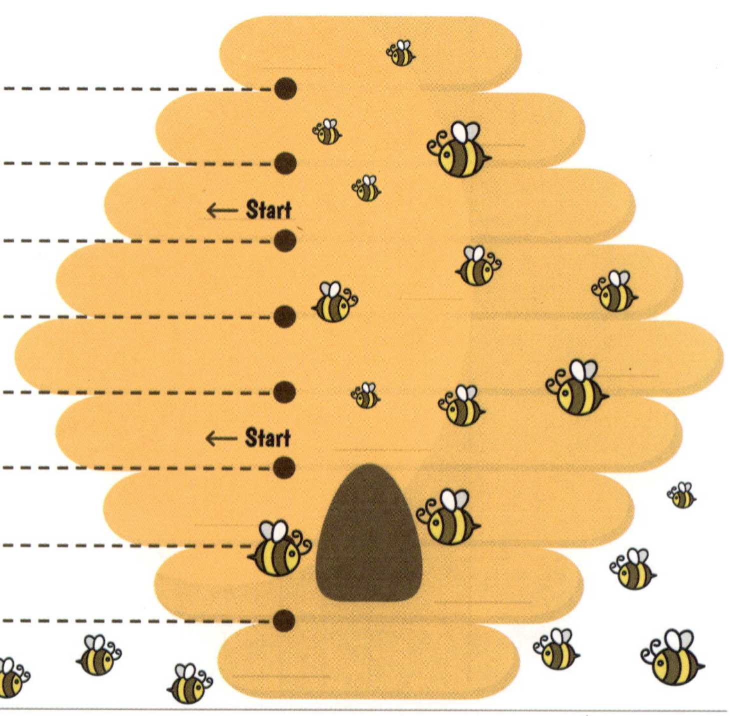

The Playful Slanting Line

Use a pencil to trace the practice lines.

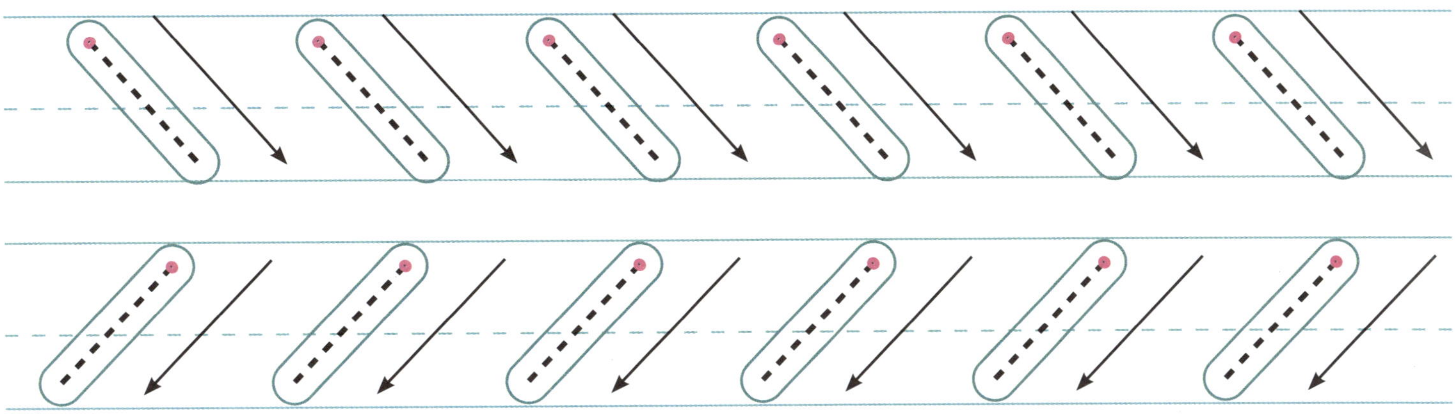

Trace the lines with your finger.

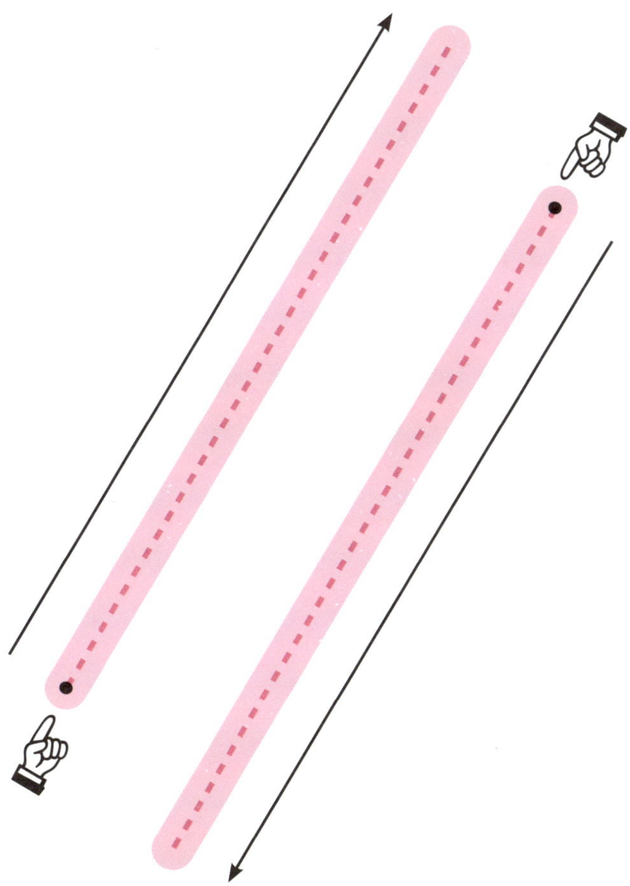

Lines

Curves That Flow

Trace the dotted, pink line with your finger.

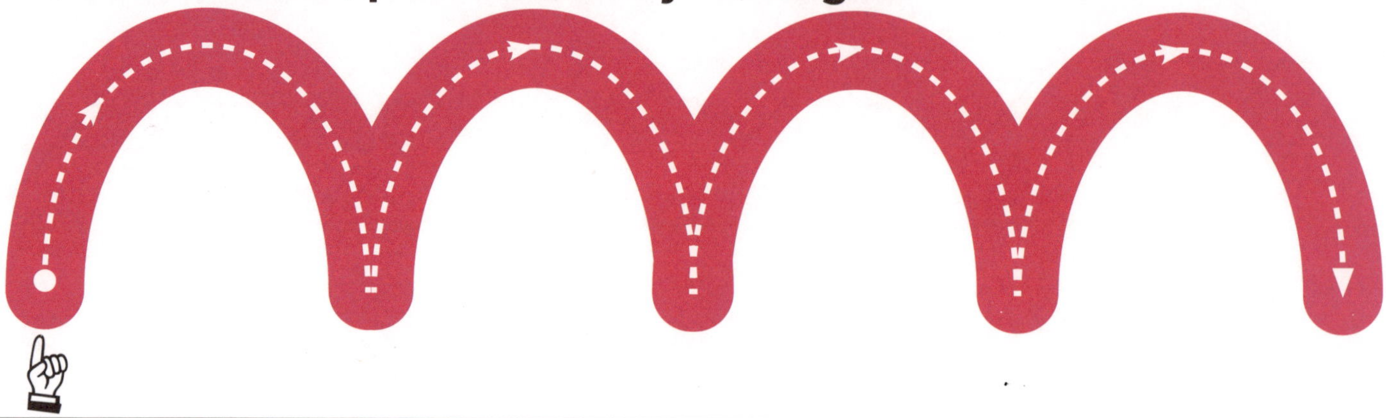

Use a pencil to trace the dotted practice lines.

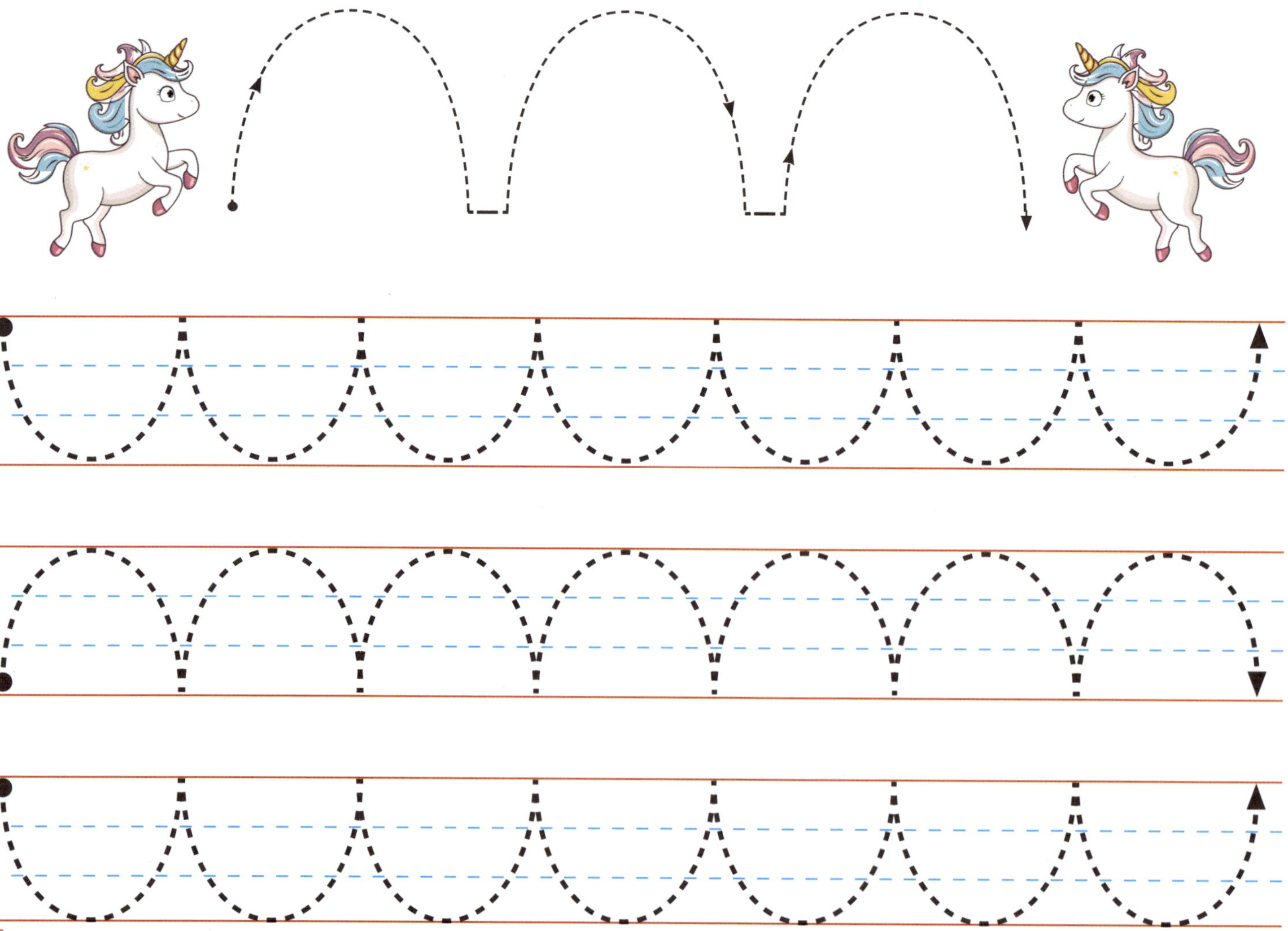

Riding the Wavy Trail

Trace the dotted, pink line with your finger.

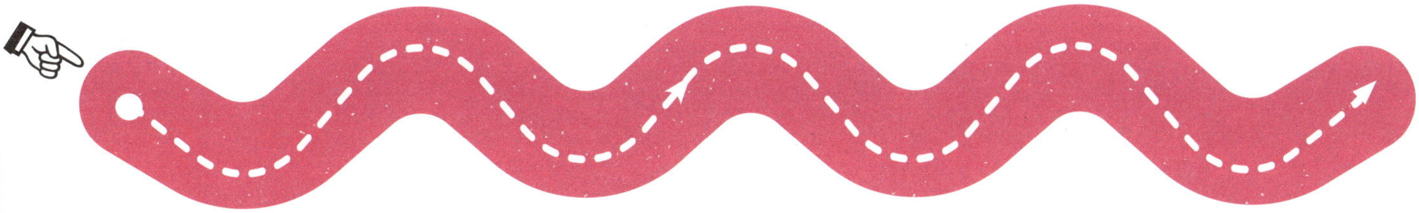

Use a pencil to trace the practice lines.

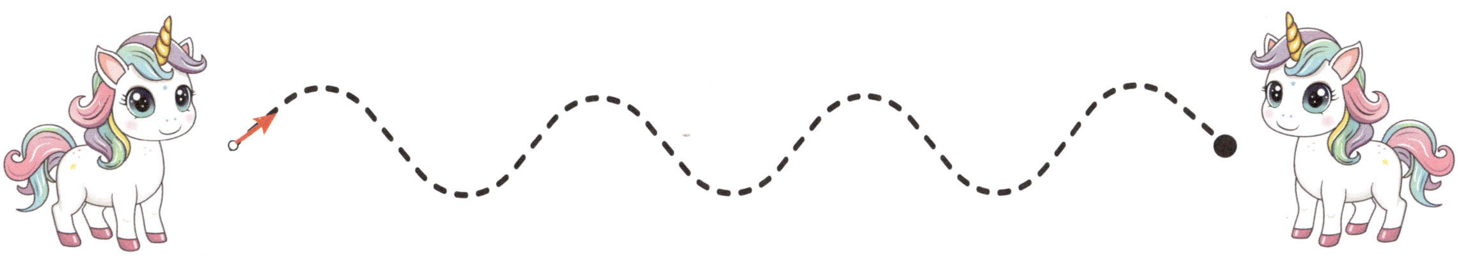

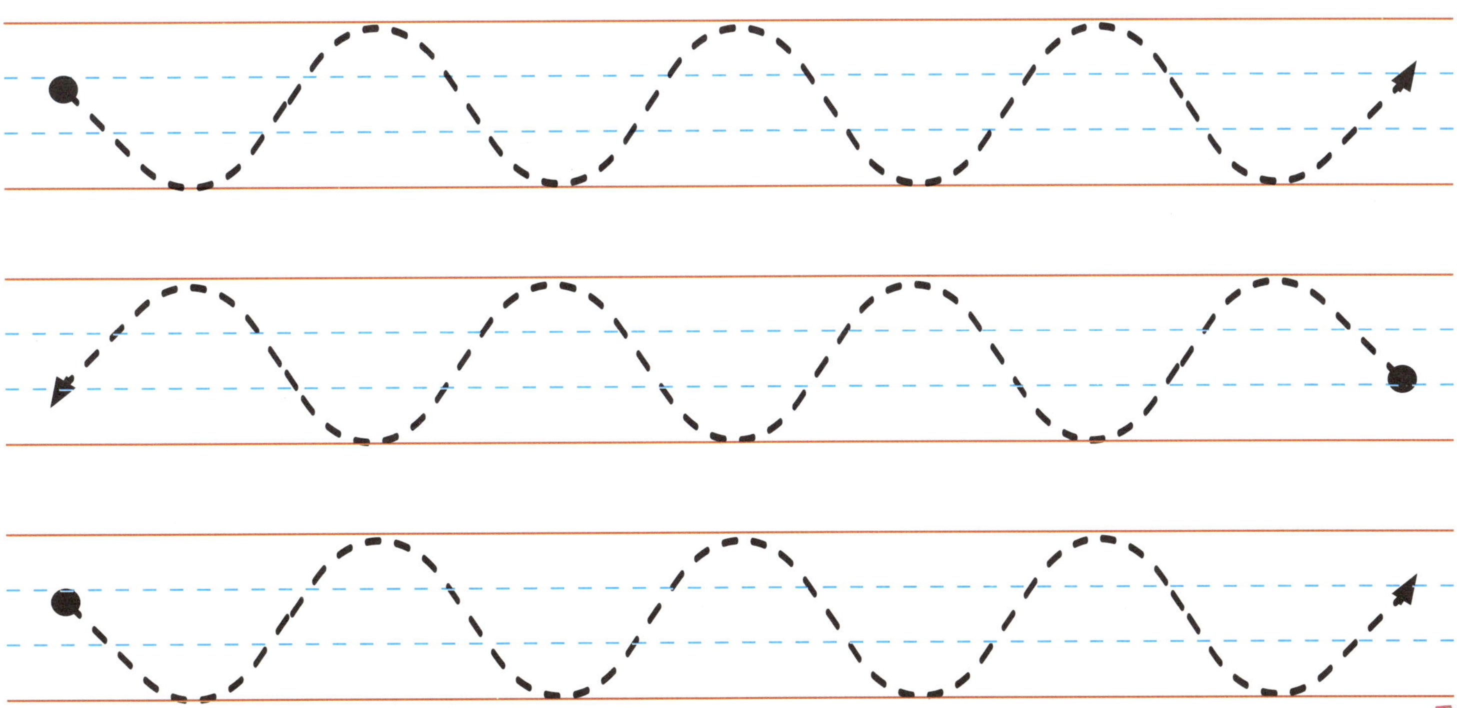

Zigzags in Action!

Trace the dotted, pink line with your finger.

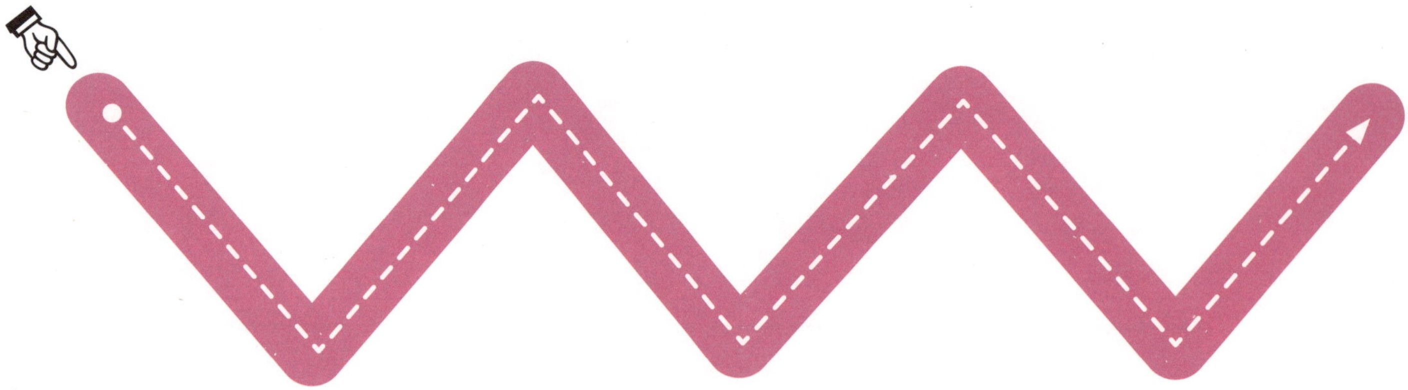

Use a pencil to trace the practice lines.

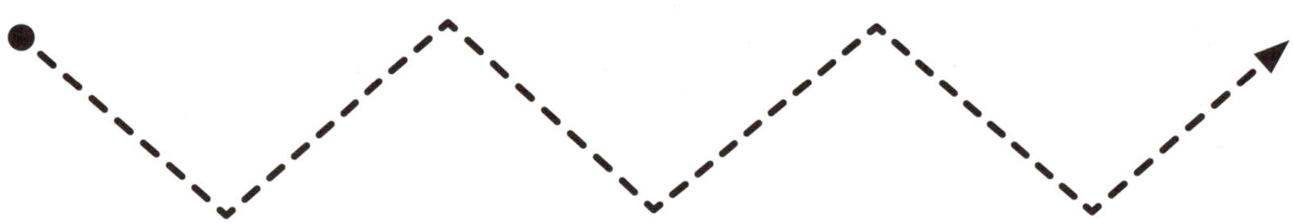

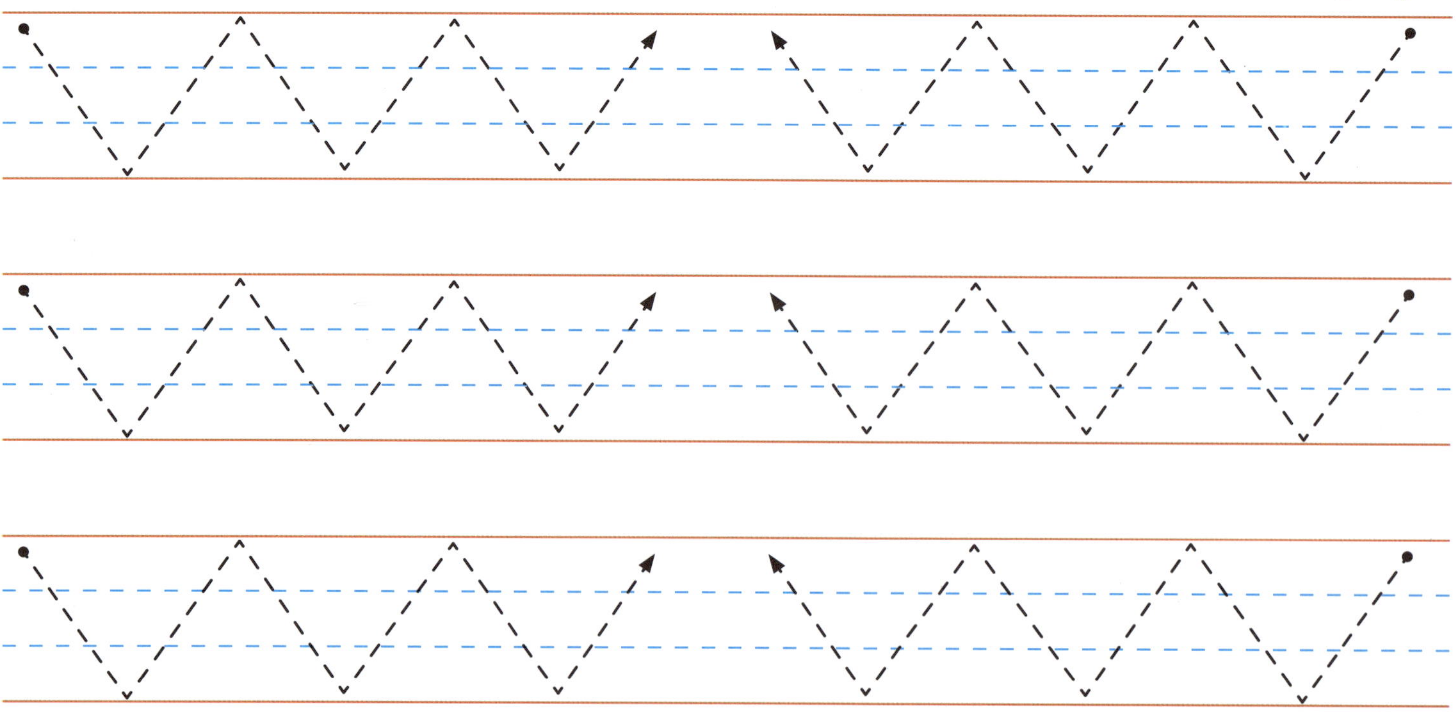

Loops That Dance

Trace the dotted, pink line with your finger.

Use a pencil to trace the practice lines.

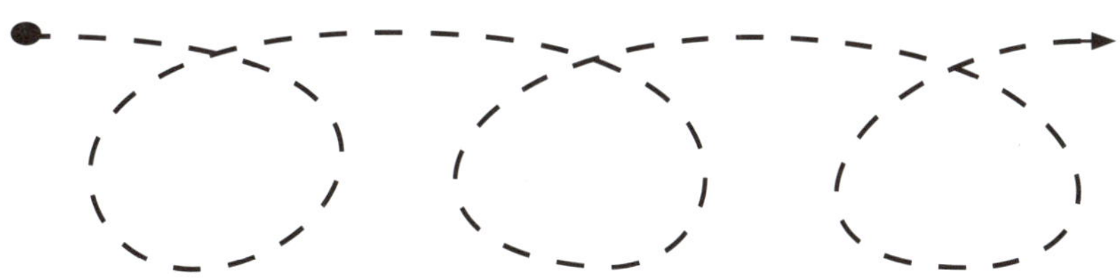

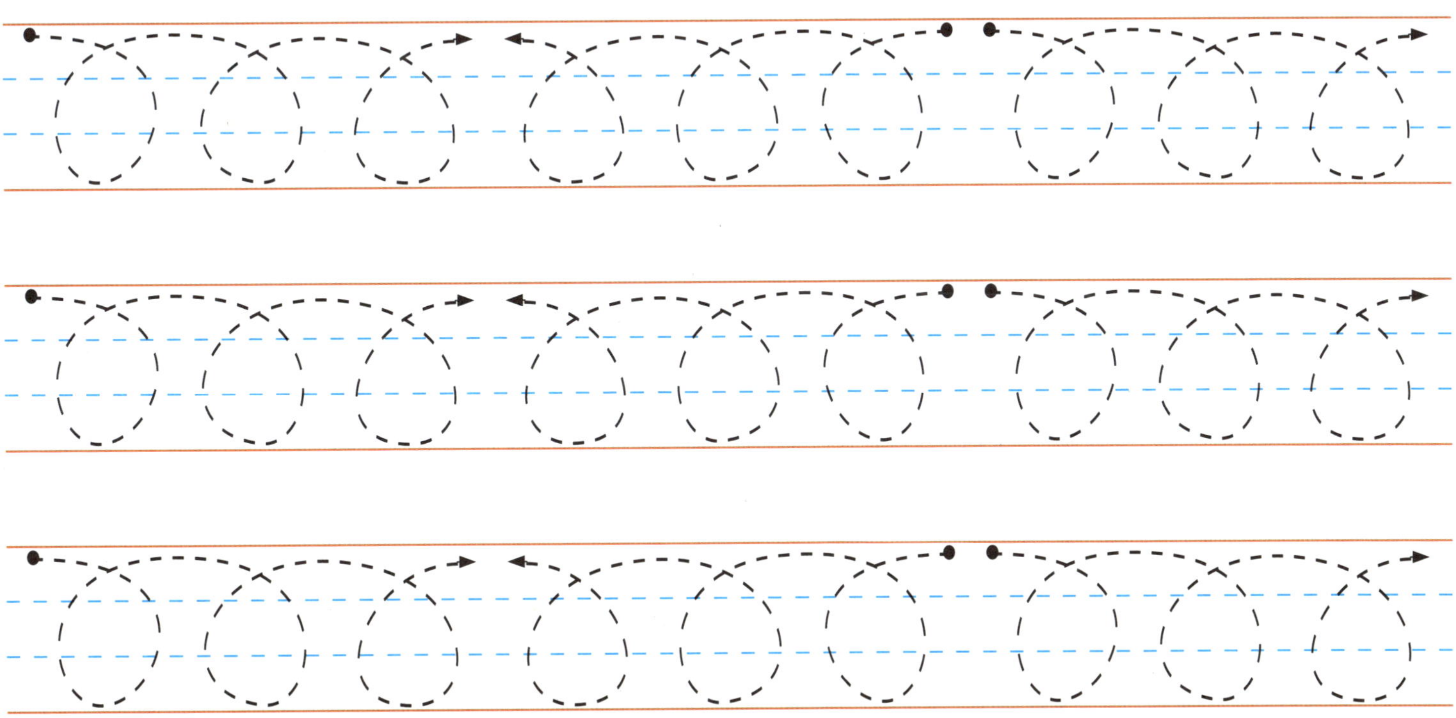

Lines

Let's Practice

Trace the practice lines in any direction.

The Perfect Circle

Trace the dotted line with your finger.

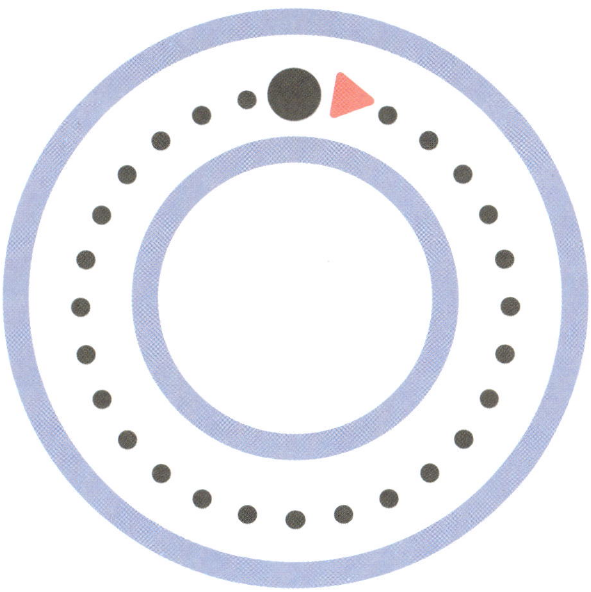

Use a pencil to trace the practice lines.

The Sturdy Square

Trace the dotted line with your finger.

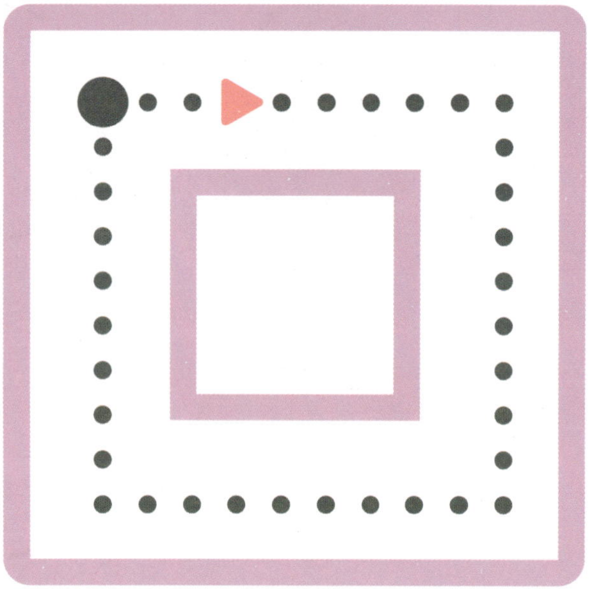

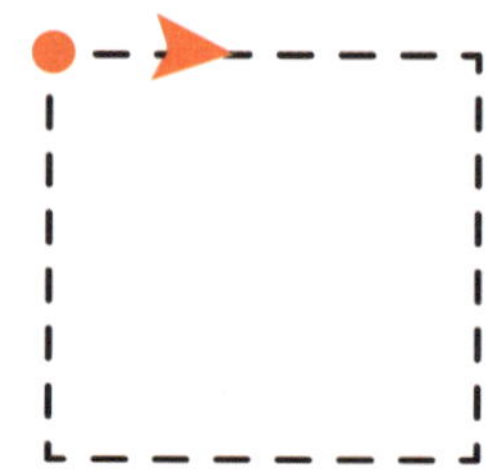

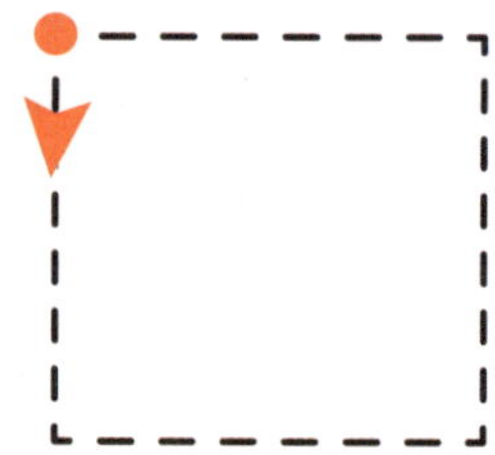

Use a pencil to trace the practice lines.

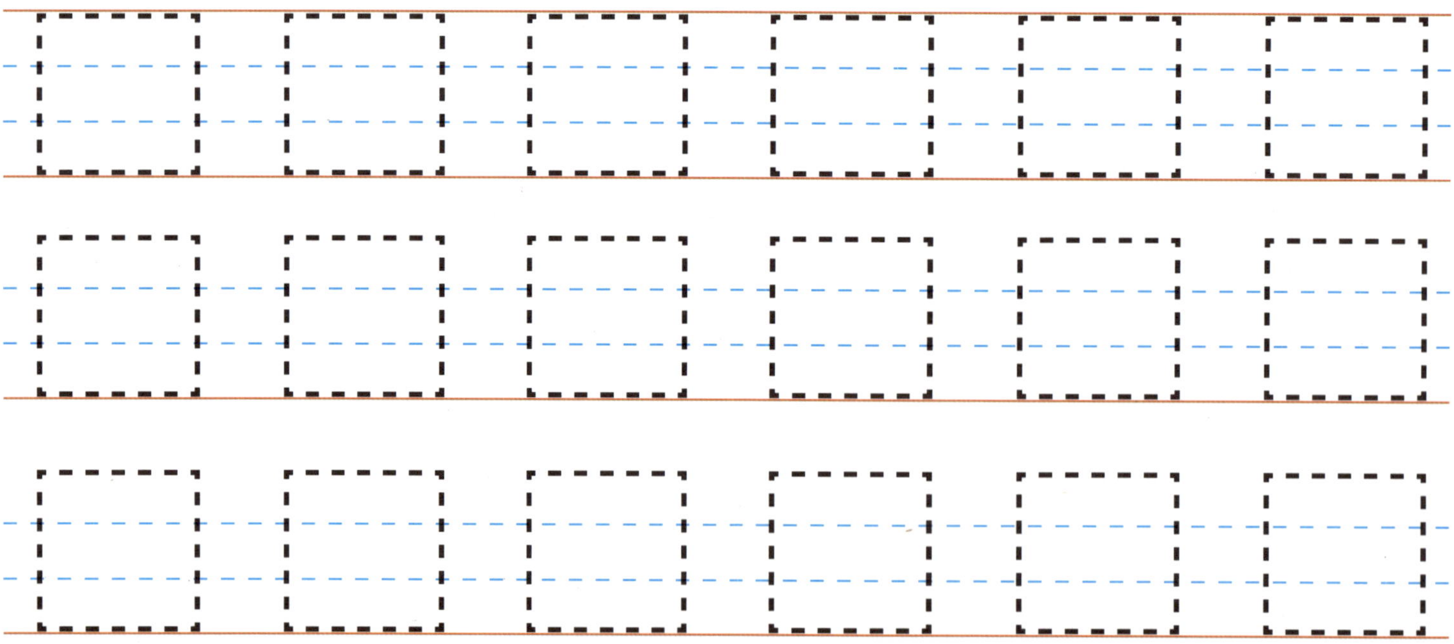

The Trusty Rectangle

Trace the dotted line with your finger.

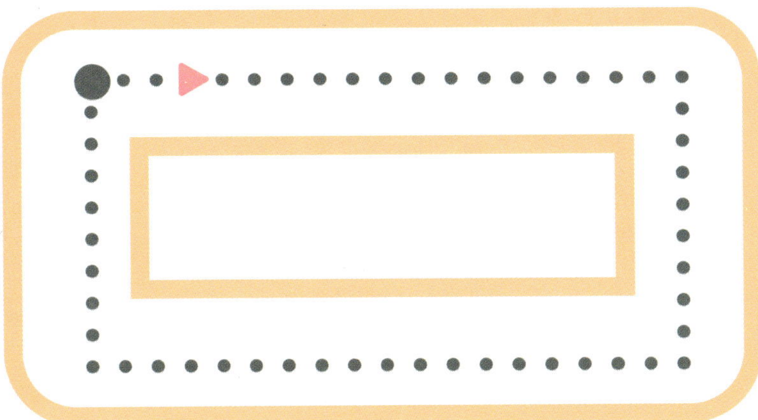

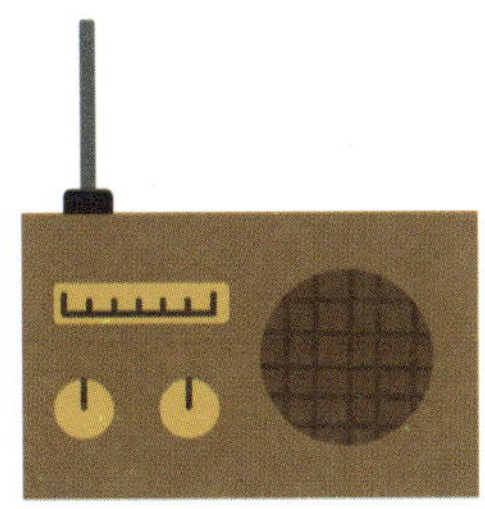

Use a pencil to trace the practice lines.

Shapes

The Smooth Oval

Trace the dotted line with your finger.

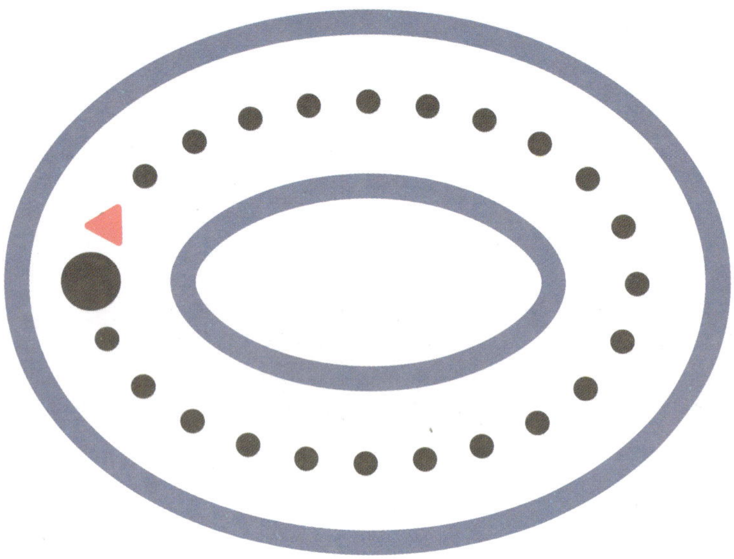

Use a pencil to trace the practice lines.

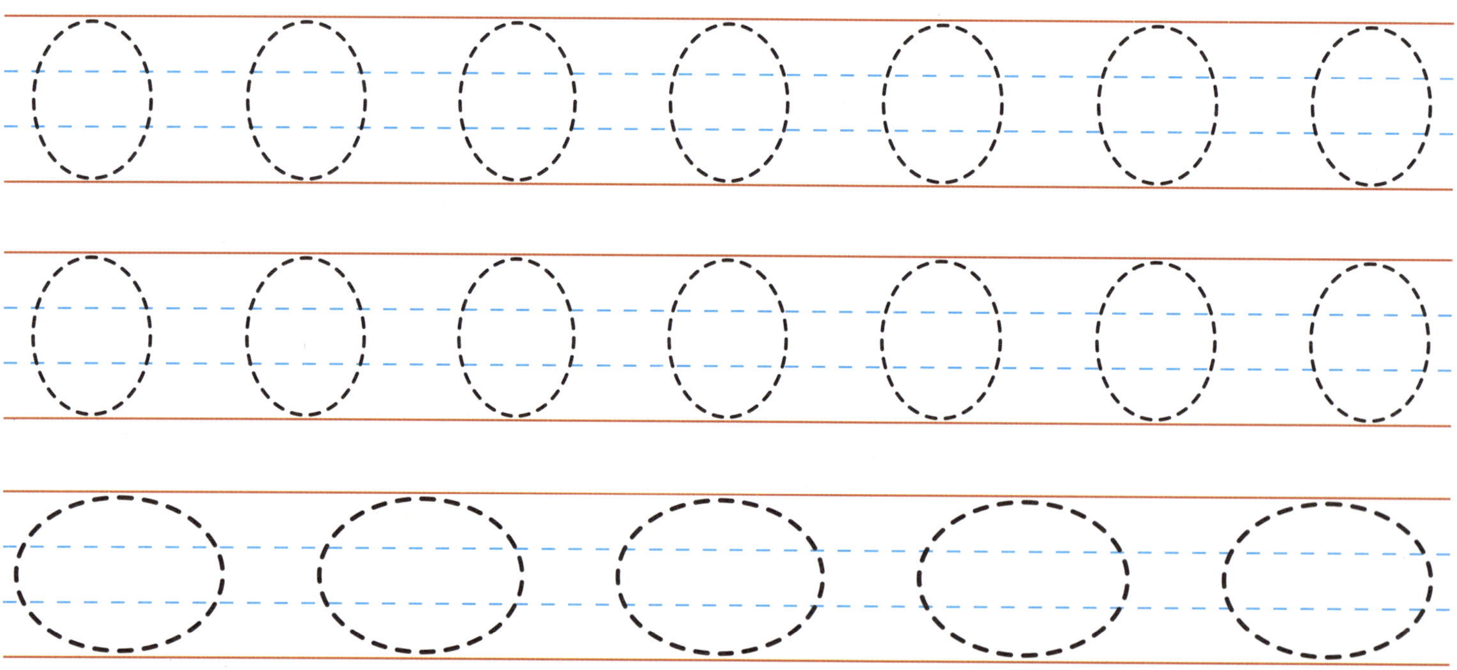

The Bold Triangle

Trace the dotted line with your finger.

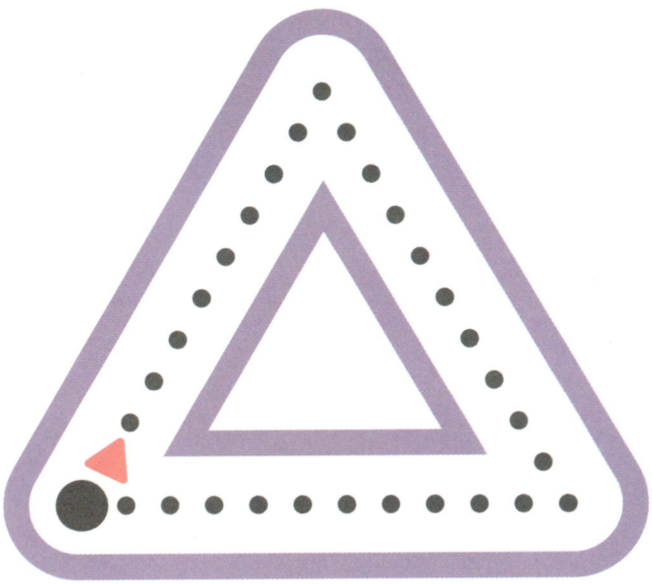

Use a pencil to trace the practice lines.

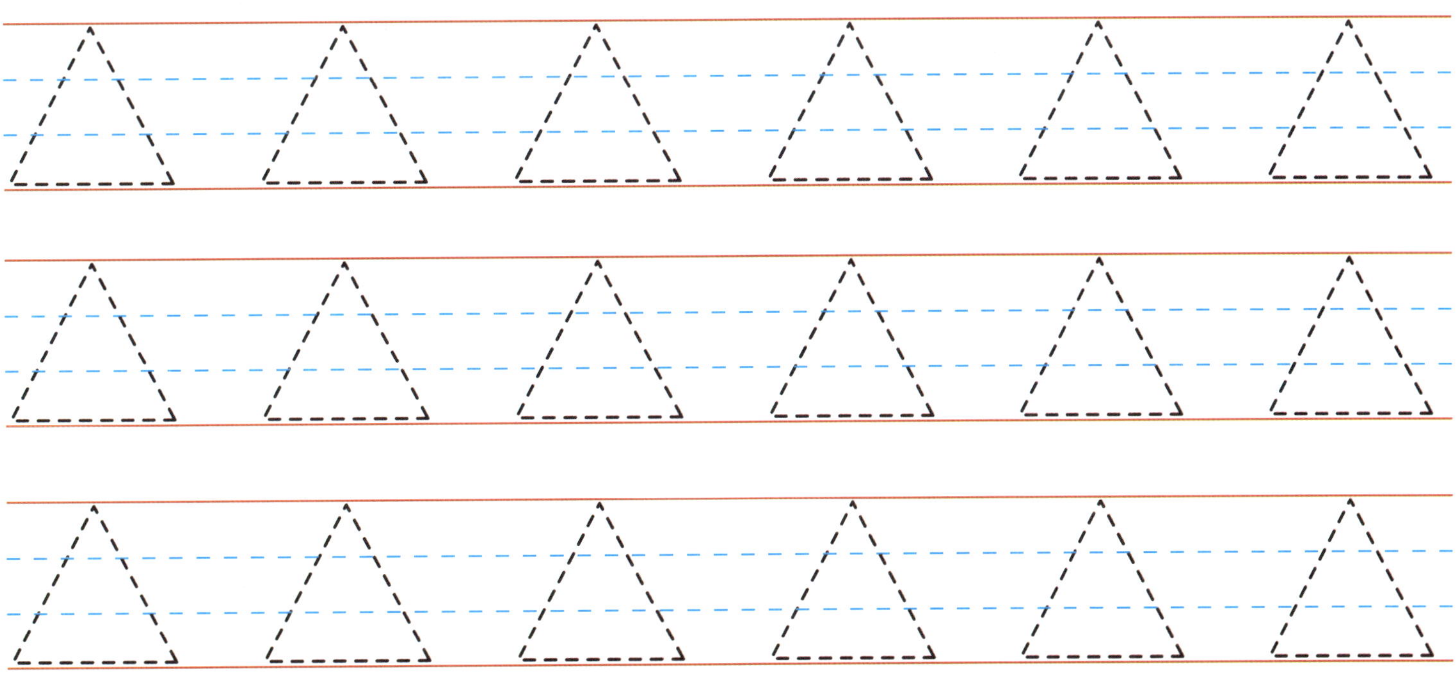

The Shiny Diamond

Trace the dotted line with your finger.

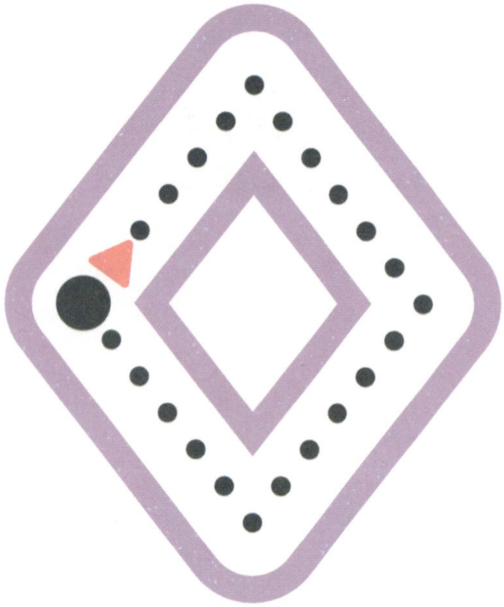

Use a pencil to trace the practice lines.

The Happy Semi-Circle

Trace the dotted line with your finger.

Use a pencil to trace the practice lines.

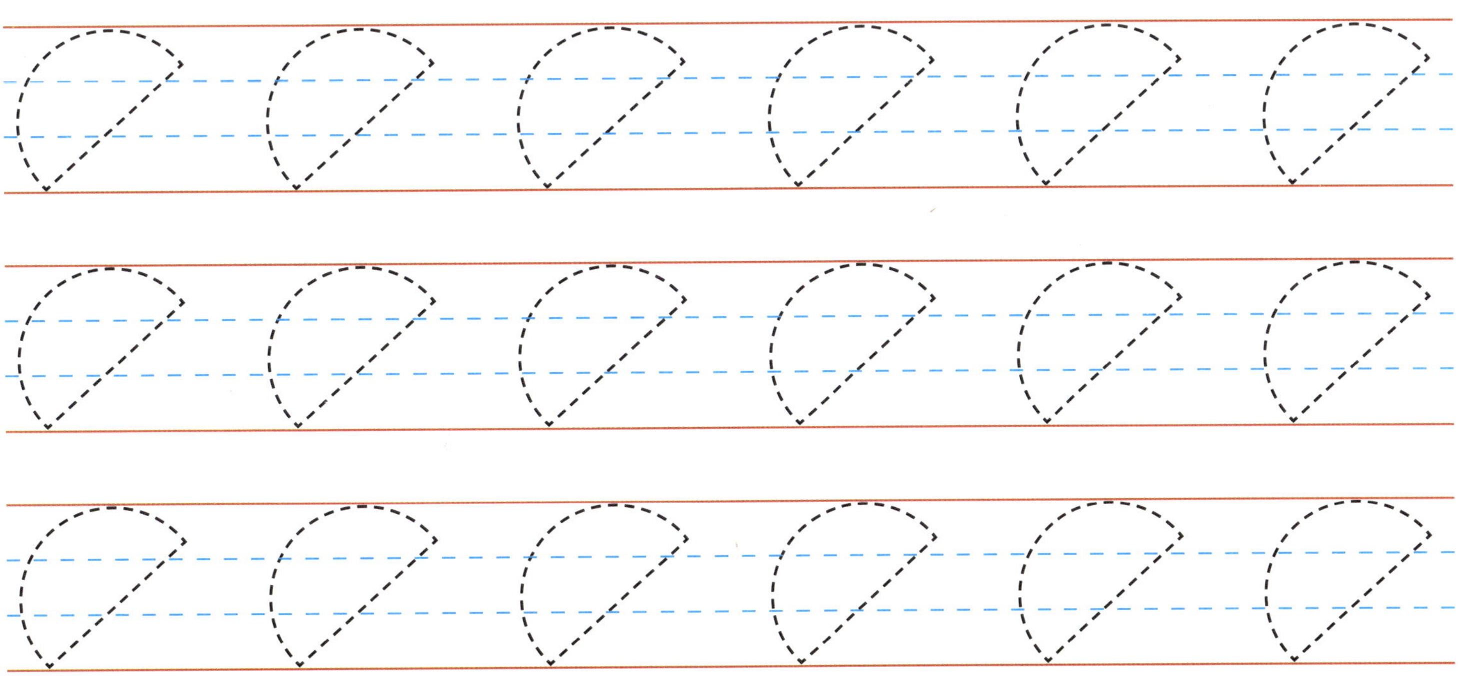

The Twinkling Star

Trace the dotted line with your finger.

Use a pencil to trace the practice lines.

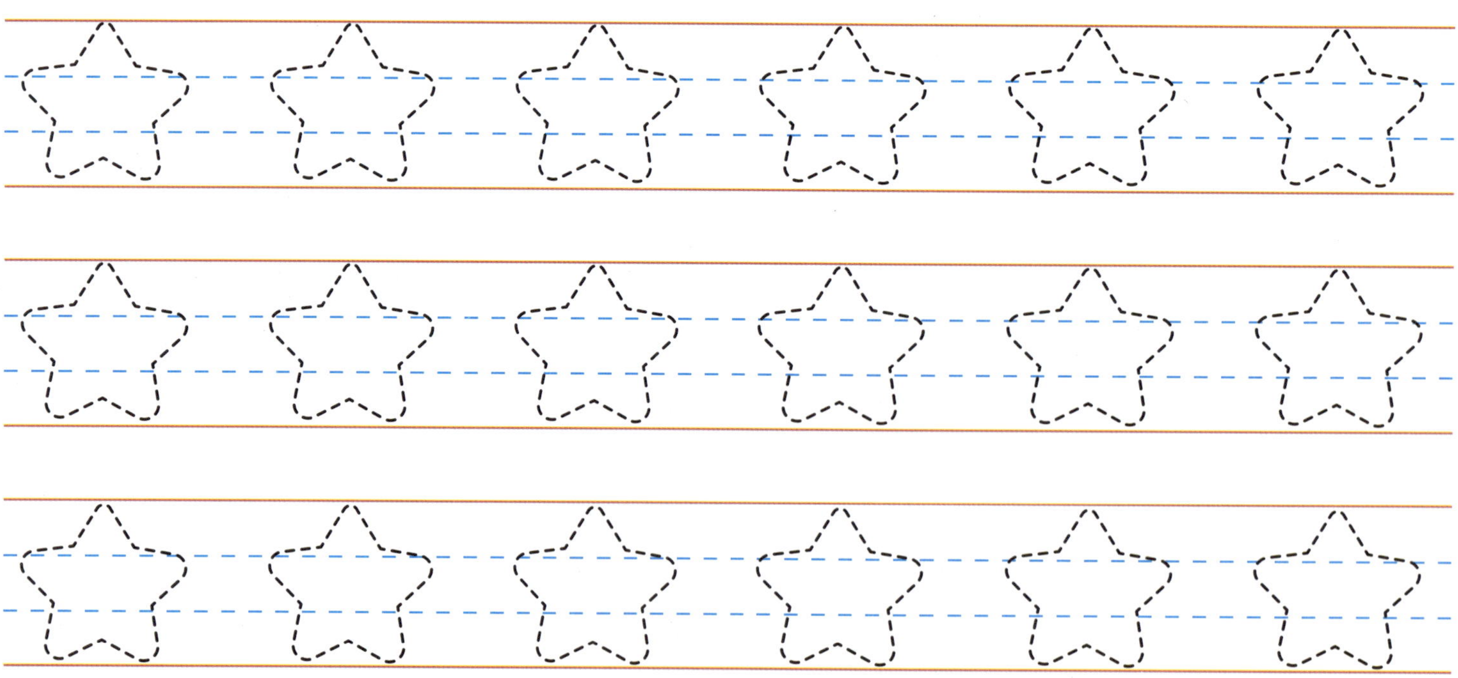

The Loving Heart

Trace the dotted line with your finger.

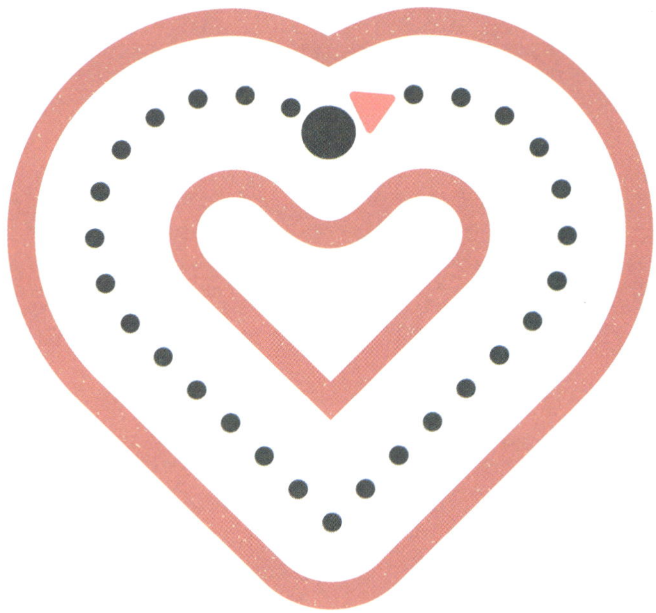

Use a pencil to trace the practice lines.

Practise, now!

Numbers

Let's Count!

Before writing numbers, get to know them first.
Use your finger to trace each number. Start with stroke 1 and continue to stroke 2.
Begin at the dot, follow the arrows and trace along the dotted lines.

Numbers

Let's Count!

Before writing numbers, get to know them first.
Use your finger to trace each number. Start with stroke 1 and continue to stroke 2.
Begin at the dot, follow the arrows and trace along the dotted lines.

Let's Count!

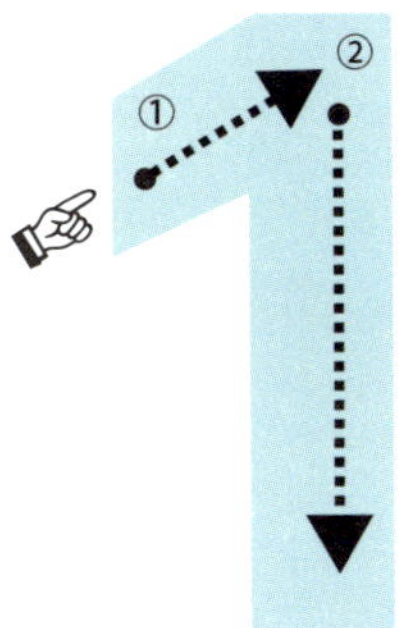

Use a pencil to trace the practice lines.

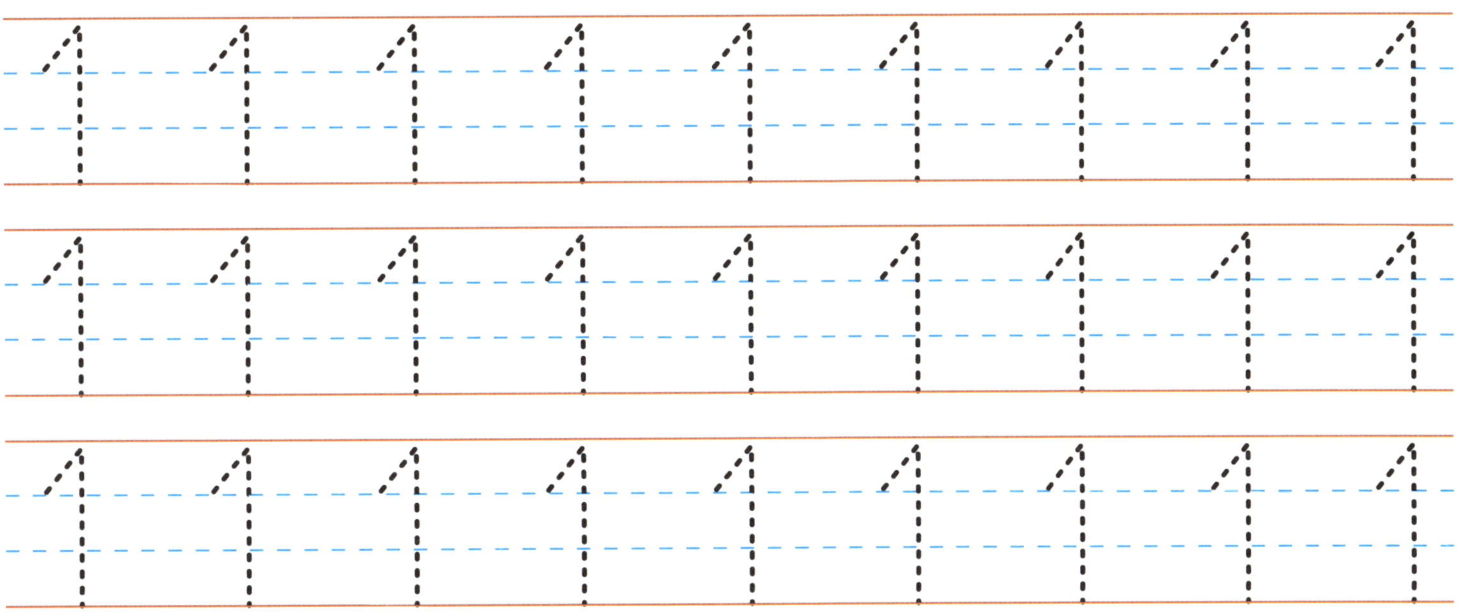

CIRCLE THE SQUARE WITH 1 UNICORN

Numbers

Let's Count!

Use a pencil to trace the practice lines.

CIRCLE THE SQUARE WITH 2 UNICORNS

Numbers

Let's Count!

Use a pencil to trace the practice lines.

CIRCLE THE SQUARE WITH 3 UNICORNS

Numbers

Let's Count!

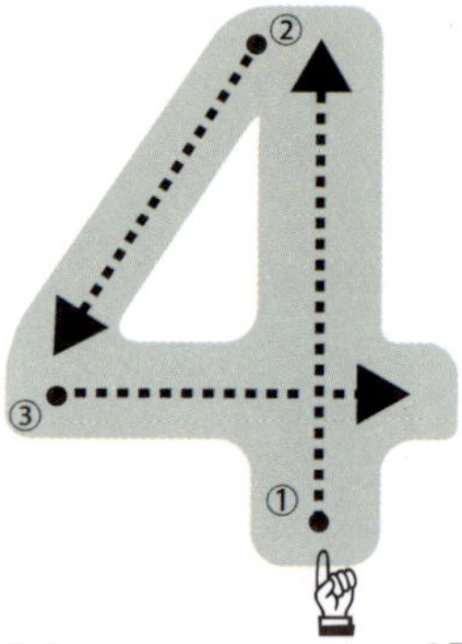

Use a pencil to trace the practice lines.

CIRCLE THE SQUARE WITH 4 UNICORNS

Let's Count!

Use a pencil to trace the practice lines.

CIRCLE THE SQUARE WITH 5 UNICORNS

Numbers

Let's Count!

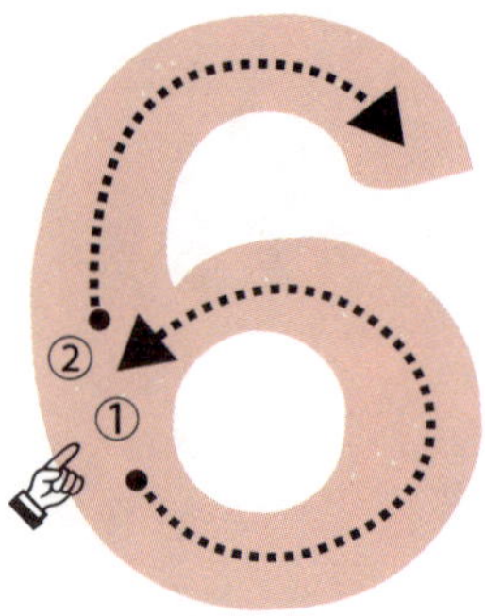

Use a pencil to trace the practice lines.

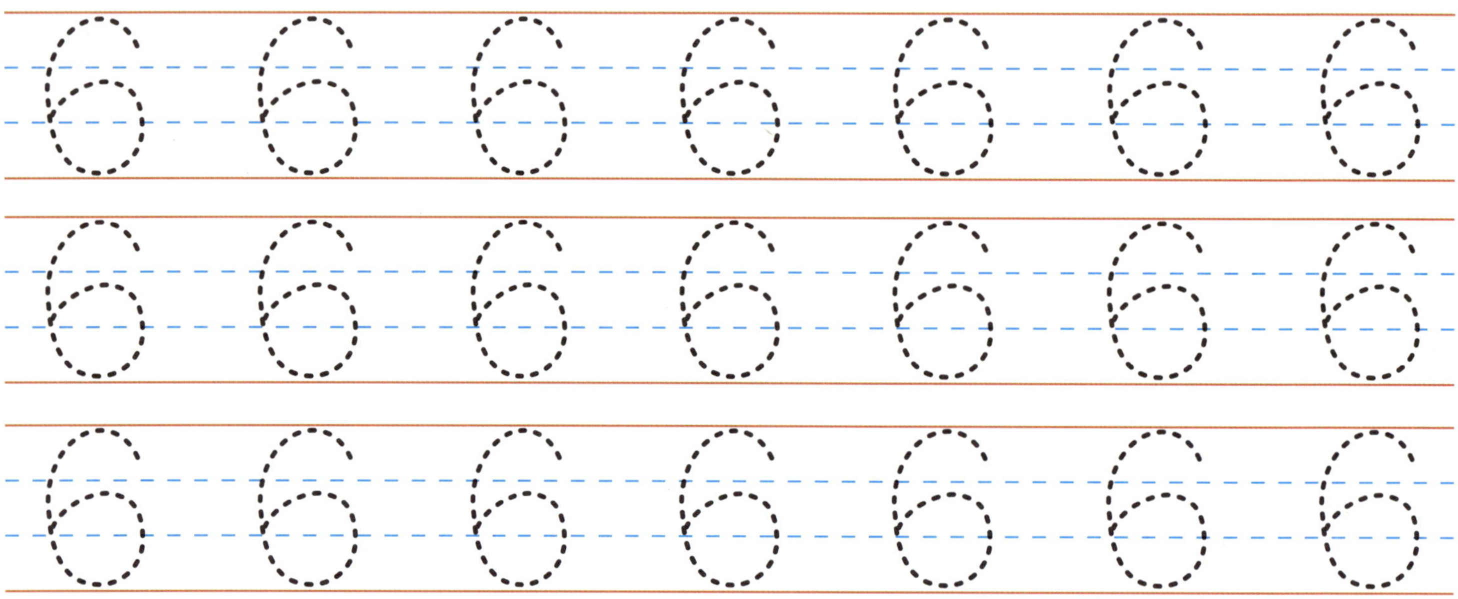

CIRCLE THE SQUARE WITH 6 UNICORNS

Numbers

Let's Count!

Use a pencil to trace the practice lines.

CIRCLE THE SQUARE WITH 7 UNICORNS

Numbers

Let's Count!

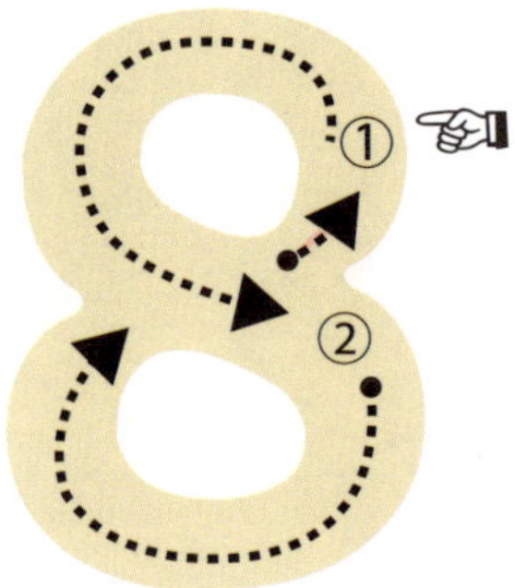

Use a pencil to trace the practice lines.

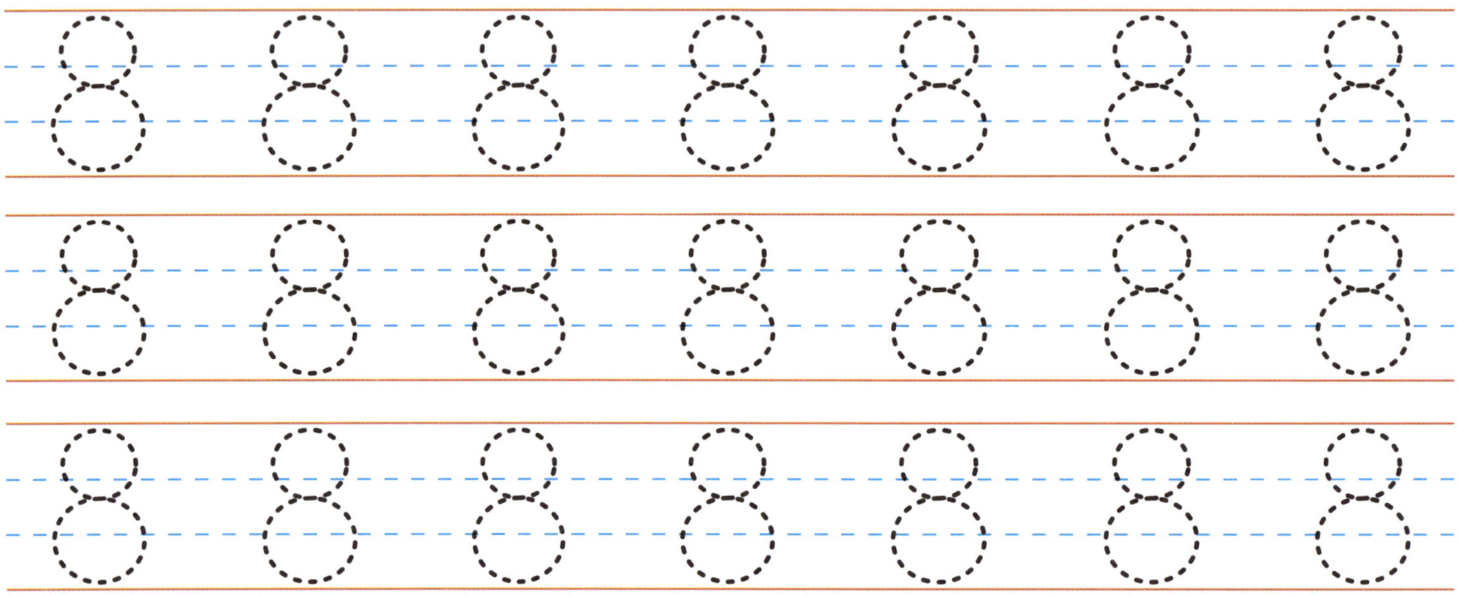

CIRCLE THE SQUARE WITH 8 UNICORNS

Let's Count!

Use a pencil to trace the practice lines.

CIRCLE THE SQUARE WITH 9 UNICORNS

Numbers

Let's Count!

Use a pencil to trace the practice lines.

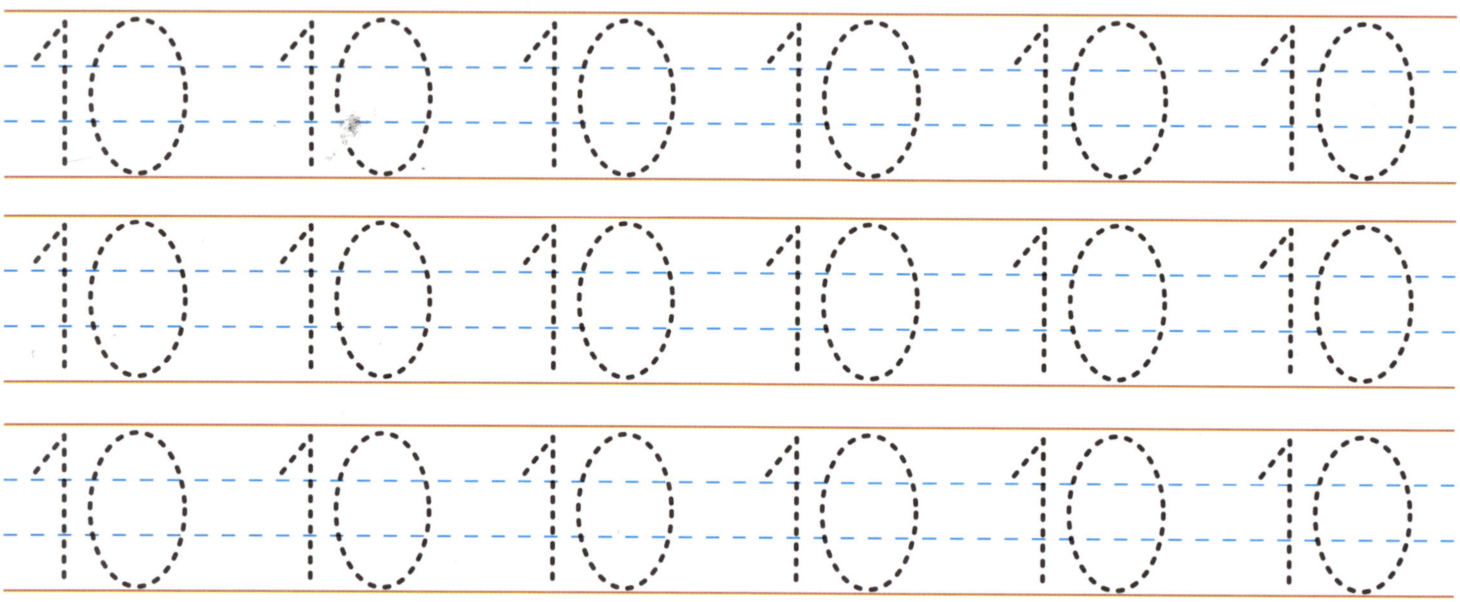

CIRCLE THE SQUARE WITH 10 UNICORNS

ABC Wonderland

Apple

Trace the lines with your finger.

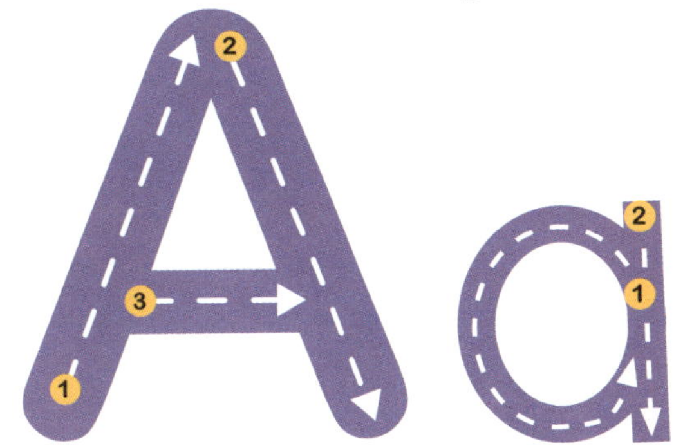

Use a pencil to trace the practice lines.

HOW MANY 'A' CAN YOU SPOT? CIRCLE THE CORRECT NUMBER COUNT!

5 3 9 1

Alphabets

ABC Wonderland

Balloon

Trace the lines with your finger.

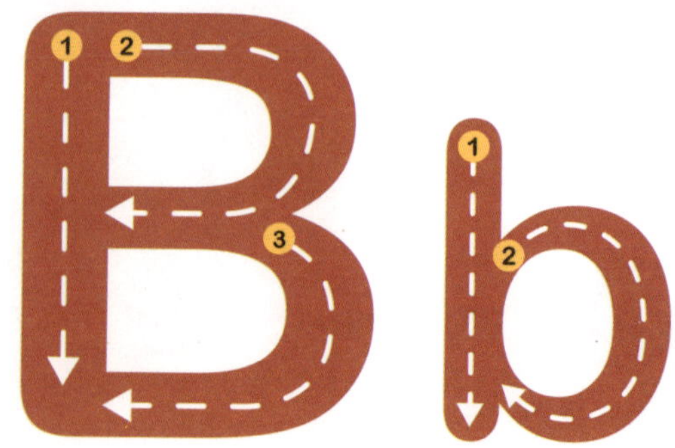

Use a pencil to trace the practice lines.

B B B B B

b b b b b b b b b b b

Bb Bb Bb Bb Bb

HOW MANY 'B' CAN YOU SPOT? CIRCLE THE CORRECT NUMBER COUNT!

6 5 4 2

ABC Wonderland

Crab

Use a pencil to trace the practice lines.

Trace the lines with your finger.

Cc

C C C C C

c c c c c c c c c c c

Cc Cc Cc Cc Cc

HOW MANY 'C' CAN YOU SPOT? CIRCLE THE CORRECT NUMBER COUNT!

1 3 6 2

Alphabets

ABC Wonderland

Dinosaur

Trace the lines with your finger.

Use a pencil to trace the practice lines.

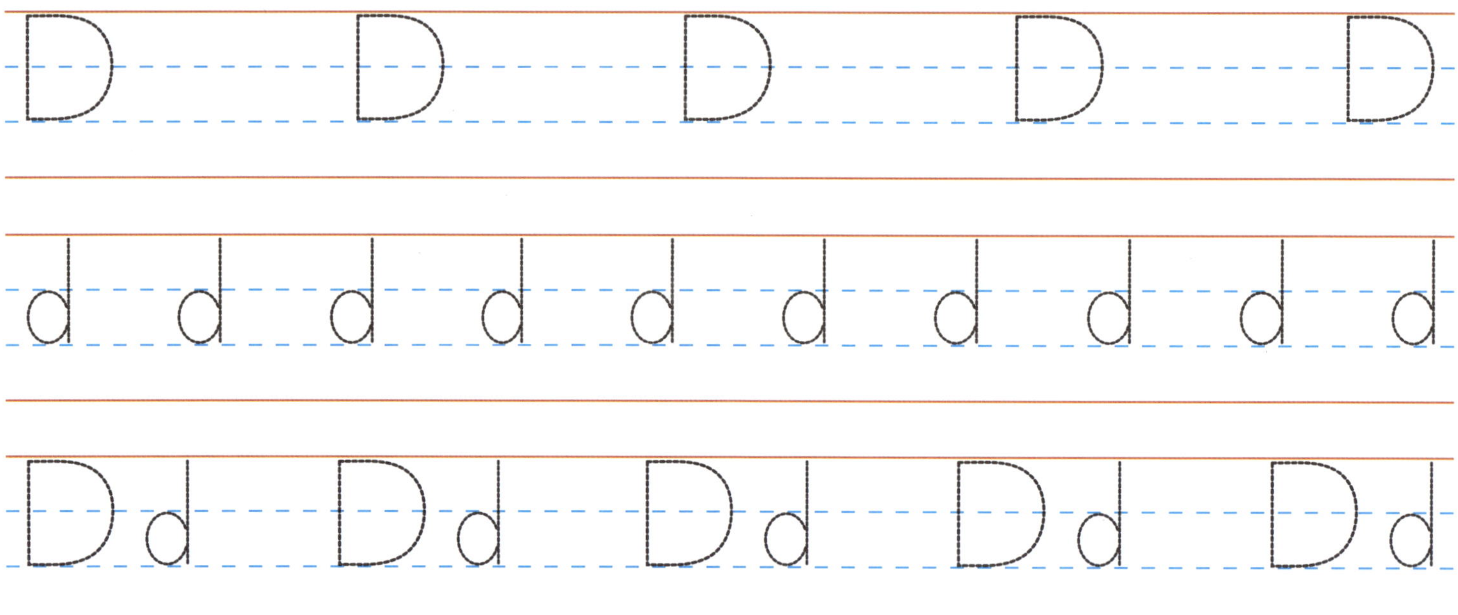

HOW MANY 'D' CAN YOU SPOT? CIRCLE THE CORRECT NUMBER COUNT!

2 4 6 7

ABC Wonderland

Eagle

Trace the lines with your finger.

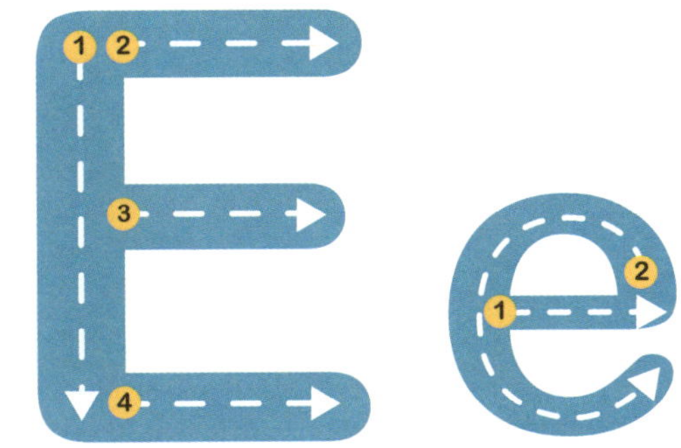

Use a pencil to trace the practice lines.

HOW MANY 'E' CAN YOU SPOT? CIRCLE THE CORRECT NUMBER COUNT!

8 6 2 4

ABC Wonderland

Fish

Use a pencil to trace the practice lines.

Trace the lines with your finger.

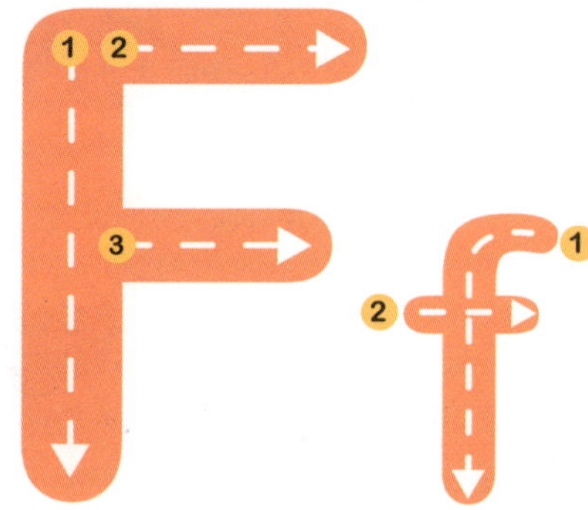

F F F F F F

f f f f f f f f f f f

Ff Ff Ff Ff Ff

HOW MANY 'F' CAN YOU SPOT? CIRCLE THE CORRECT NUMBER COUNT!

3 1 4 5

ABC Wonderland

Trace the lines with your finger.

Use a pencil to trace the practice lines.

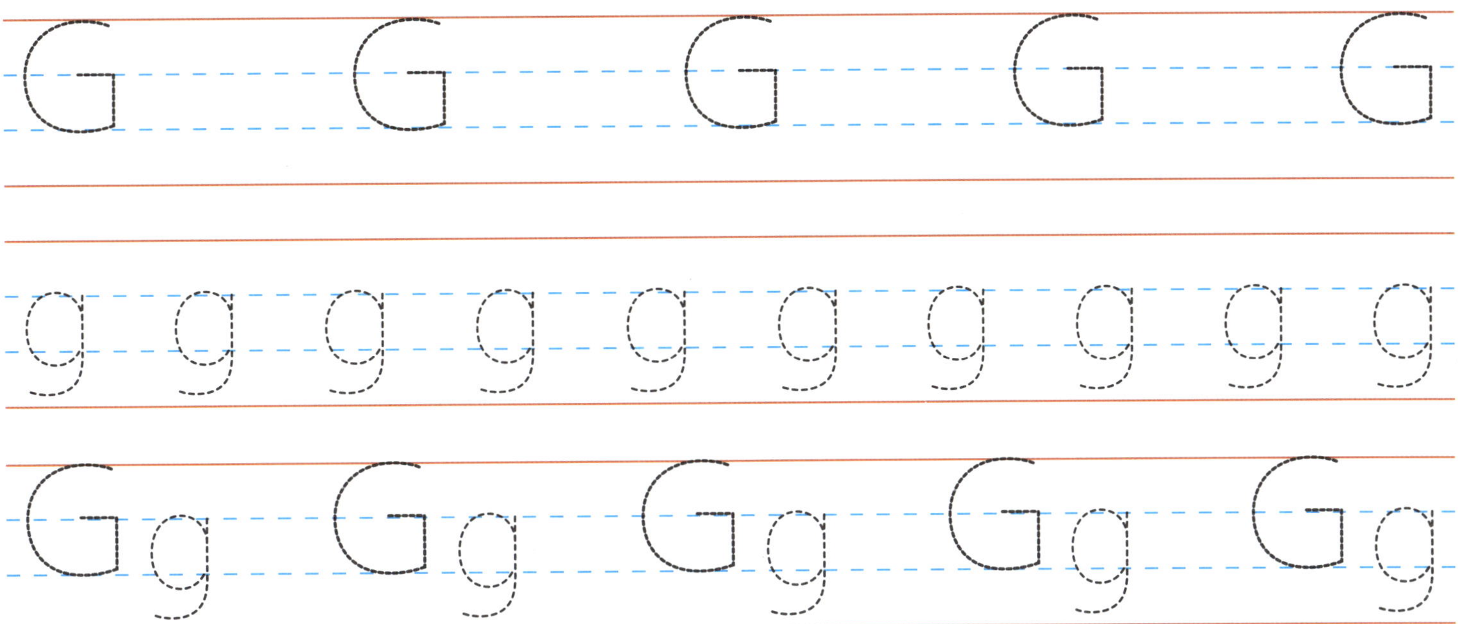

HOW MANY 'G' CAN YOU SPOT? CIRCLE THE CORRECT NUMBER COUNT!

3 2 4 1

Alphabets

ABC Wonderland

Horse

Use a pencil to trace the practice lines.

Trace the lines with your finger.

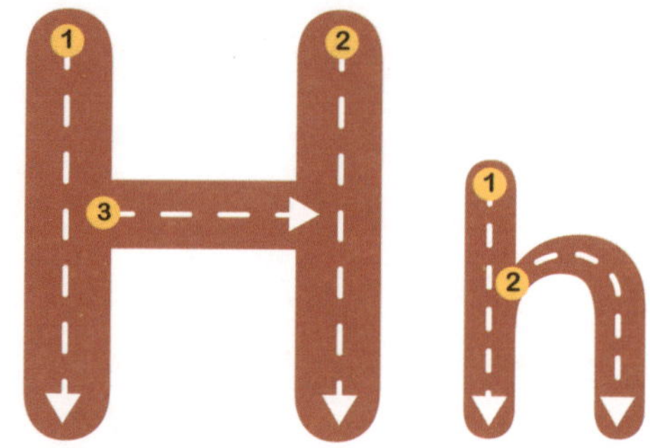

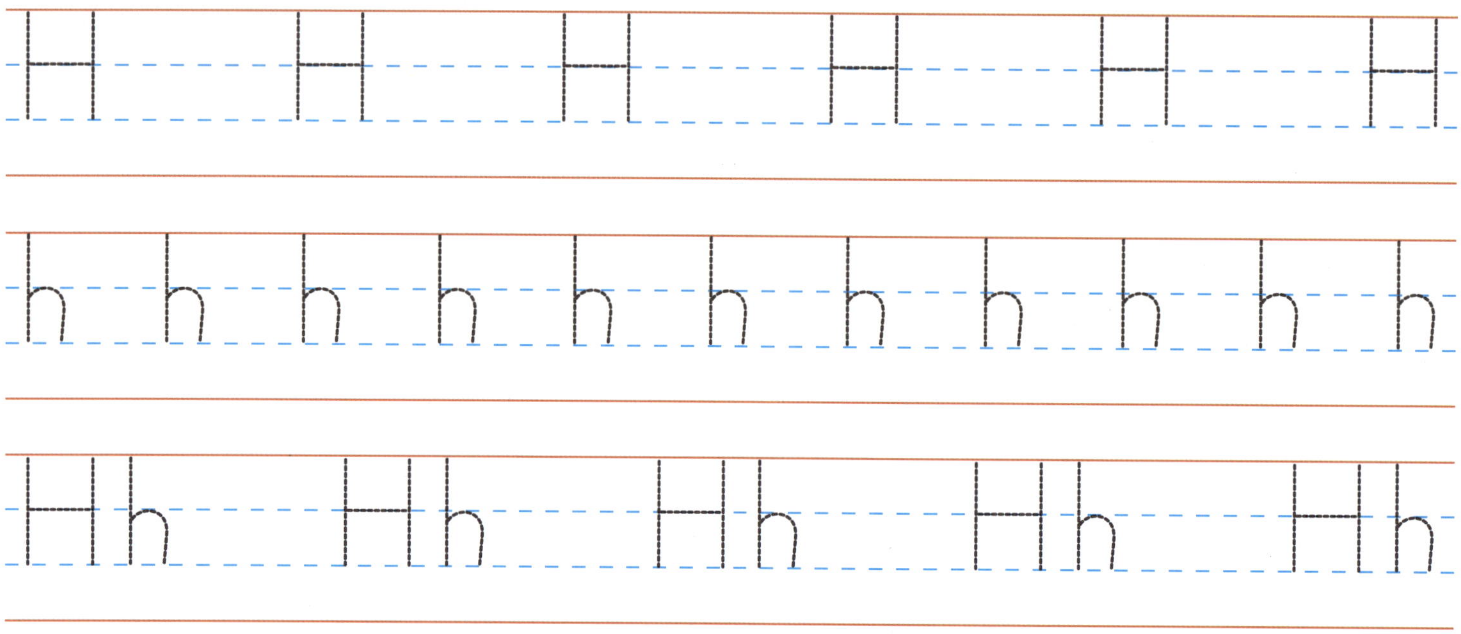

HOW MANY 'H' CAN YOU SPOT?
CIRCLE THE CORRECT NUMBER COUNT!

5 1 4 9

ABC Wonderland

Igloo

Trace the lines with your finger.

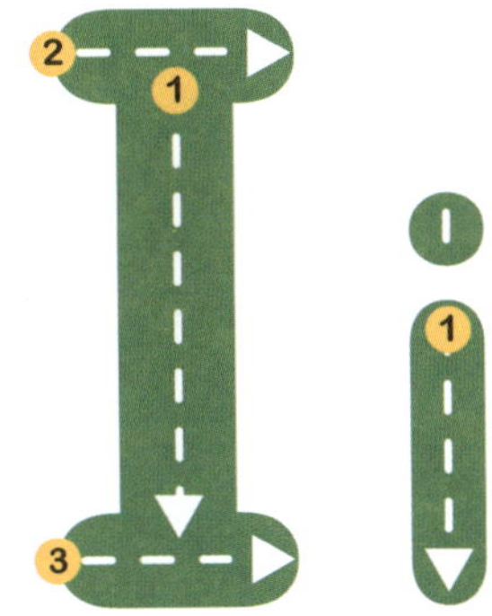

Use a pencil to trace the practice lines.

HOW MANY 'I' CAN YOU SPOT? CIRCLE THE CORRECT NUMBER COUNT!

1 9 4 0

ABC Wonderland

Jam

Use a pencil to trace the practice lines.

Trace the lines with your finger.

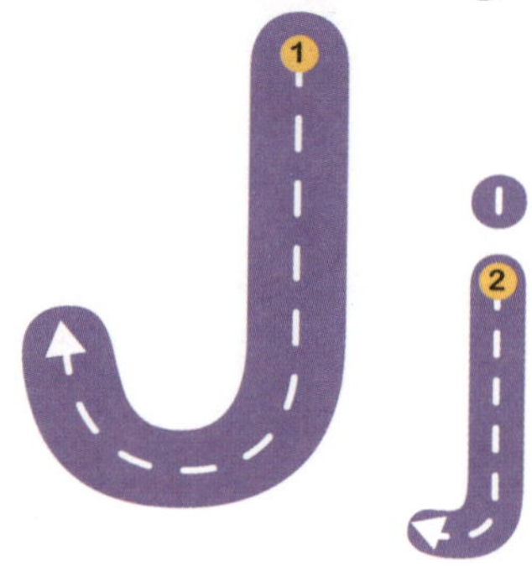

HOW MANY 'J' CAN YOU SPOT? CIRCLE THE CORRECT NUMBER COUNT!

1 9 3 5

ABC Wonderland

Kite

Use a pencil to trace the practice lines.

Trace the lines with your finger.

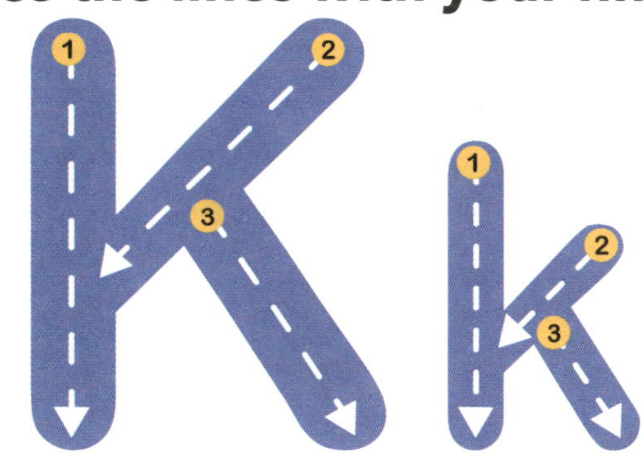

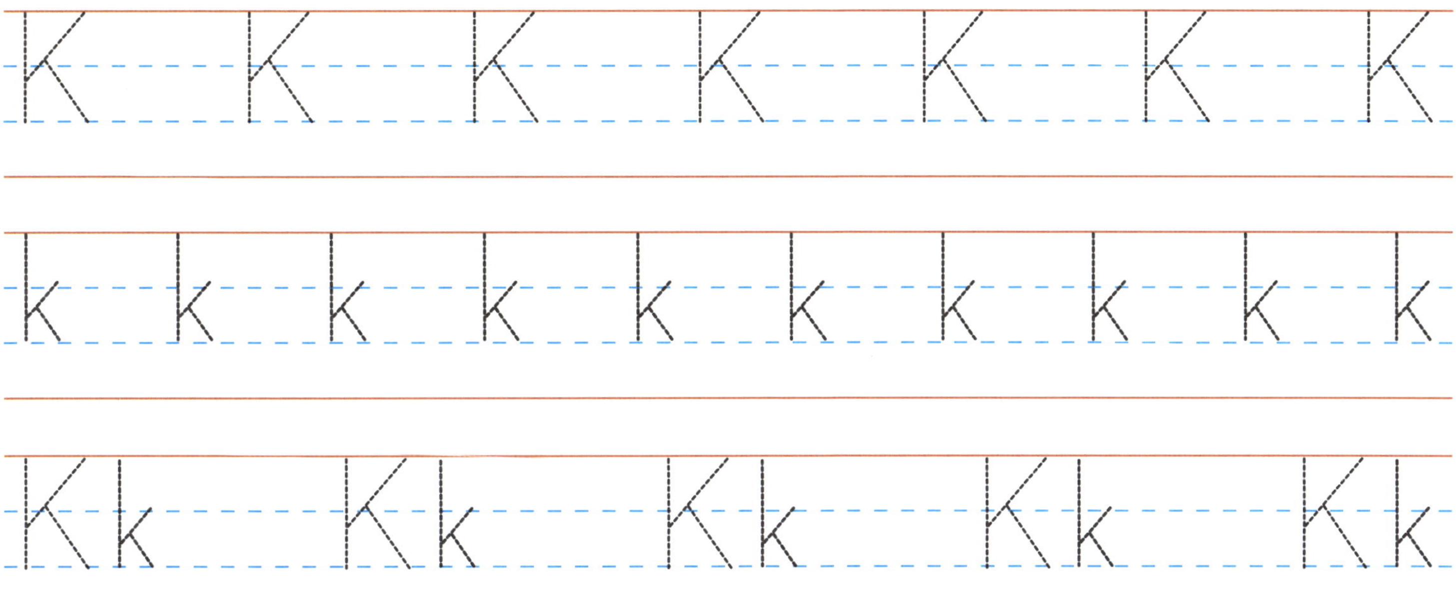

HOW MANY 'K' CAN YOU SPOT? CIRCLE THE CORRECT NUMBER COUNT!

1 5 8 6

Alphabets

ABC Wonderland

Lemur

Use a pencil to trace the practice lines.

Trace the lines with your finger.

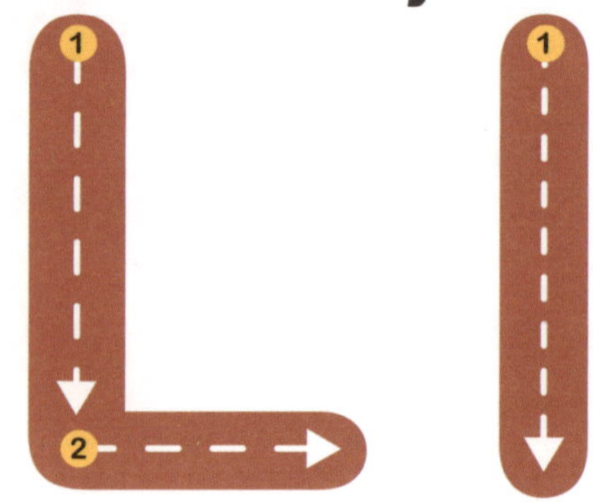

HOW MANY 'L' CAN YOU SPOT? CIRCLE THE CORRECT NUMBER COUNT!

9 8 3 0

ABC Wonderland

Mouse

Use a pencil to trace the practice lines.

Trace the lines with your finger.

M m

M M M M M M

m m m m m m m m m m m

Mm Mm Mm Mm Mm

HOW MANY 'M' CAN YOU SPOT? CIRCLE THE CORRECT NUMBER COUNT!

3 0 1 5

Alphabets

ABC Wonderland

Night

Use a pencil to trace the practice lines.

Trace the lines with your finger.

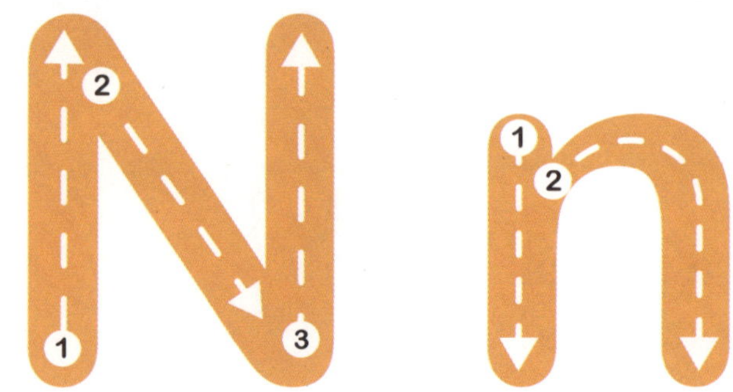

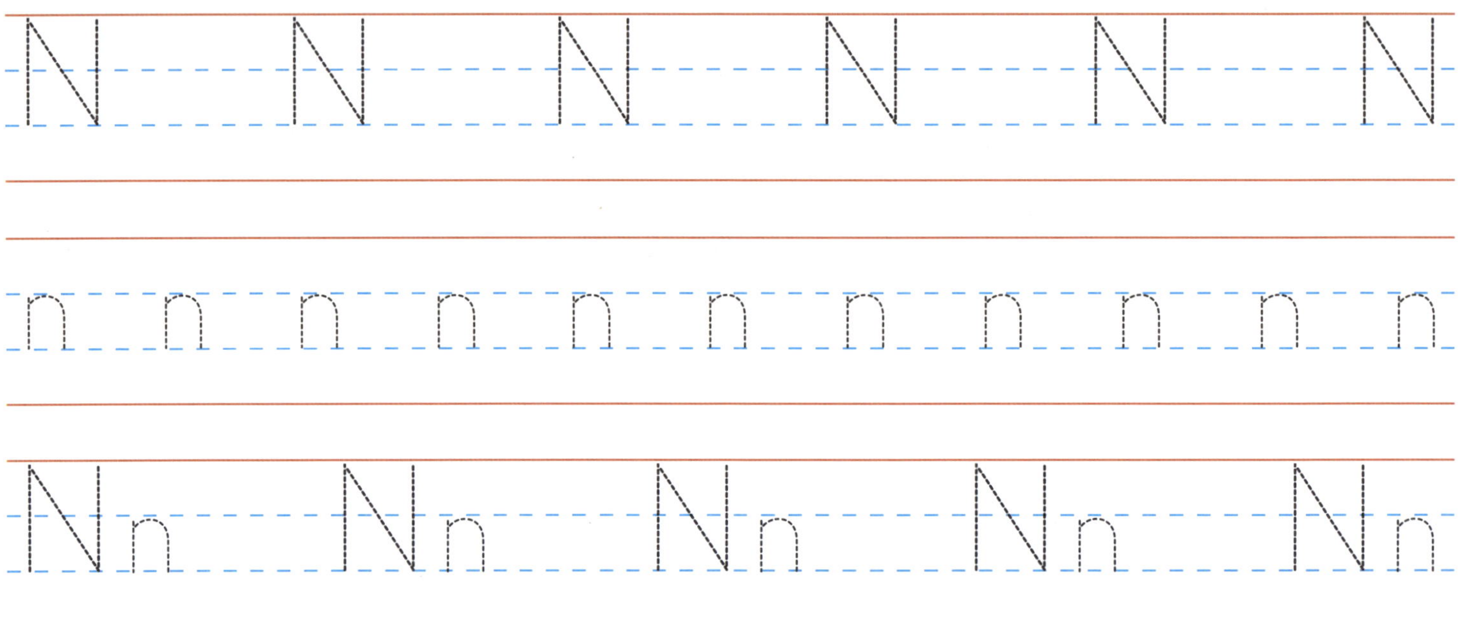

HOW MANY 'N' CAN YOU SPOT? CIRCLE THE CORRECT NUMBER COUNT!

5 4 8 1

ABC Wonderland

Owl

Use a pencil to trace the practice lines.

Trace the lines with your finger.

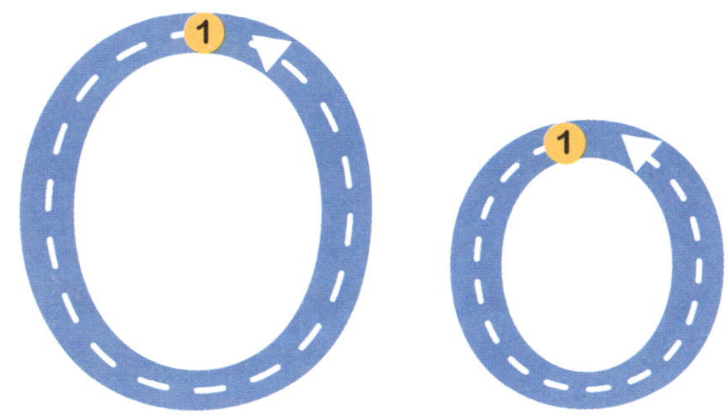

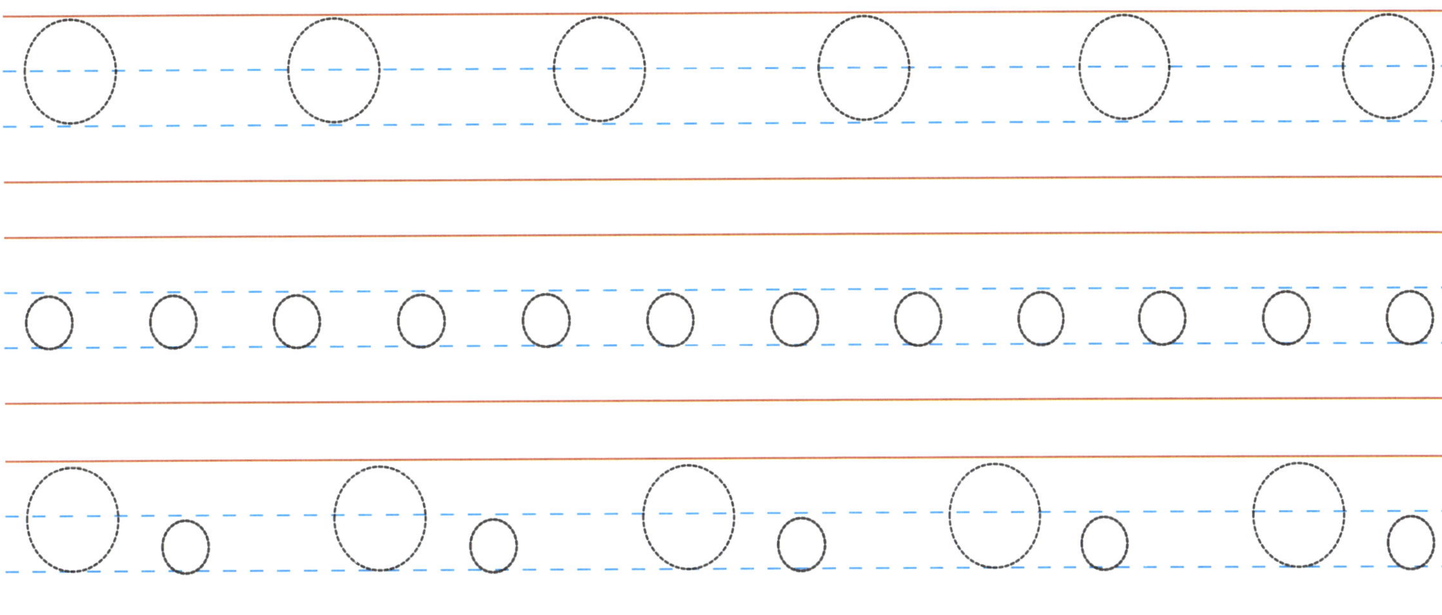

HOW MANY 'O' CAN YOU SPOT? CIRCLE THE CORRECT NUMBER COUNT!

5 7 1 2

ABC Wonderland

Pig

Trace the lines with your finger.

Use a pencil to trace the practice lines.

HOW MANY 'P' CAN YOU SPOT? CIRCLE THE CORRECT NUMBER COUNT!

0 1 9 2

ABC Wonderland

Queen

Use a pencil to trace the practice lines.

Trace the lines with your finger.

HOW MANY 'Q' CAN YOU SPOT? CIRCLE THE CORRECT NUMBER COUNT!

2 1 7 3

Alphabets

ABC Wonderland

Trace the lines with your finger.

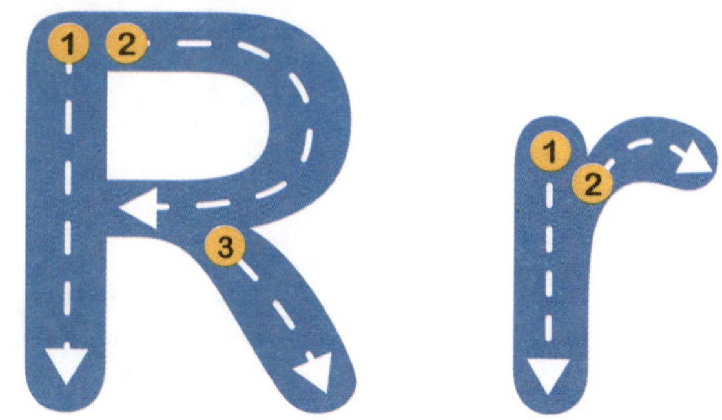

Rocket

Use a pencil to trace the practice lines.

R R R R R R R R

r r r r r r r r r r r

Rr Rr Rr Rr Rr Rr

HOW MANY 'R' CAN YOU SPOT? CIRCLE THE CORRECT NUMBER COUNT!

6 1 9 8

ABC Wonderland

Squirrel

Use a pencil to trace the practice lines.

Trace the lines with your finger.

Ss

HOW MANY 'S' CAN YOU SPOT? CIRCLE THE CORRECT NUMBER COUNT!

9 6 4 3

Alphabets

ABC Wonderland

Trace the lines with your finger.

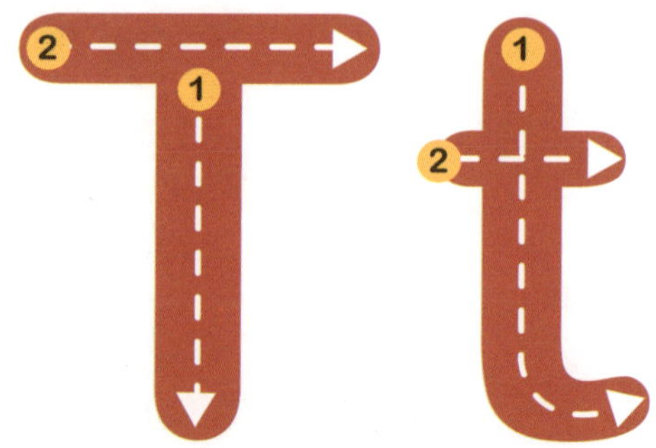

Turtle

Use a pencil to trace the practice lines.

HOW MANY 'T' CAN YOU SPOT? CIRCLE THE CORRECT NUMBER COUNT!

1 6 4 9

ABC Wonderland

Unicorn

Trace the lines with your finger.

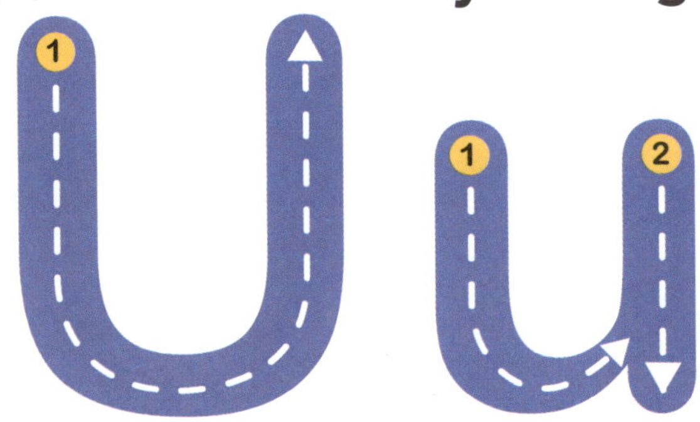

Use a pencil to trace the practice lines.

HOW MANY 'U' CAN YOU SPOT? CIRCLE THE CORRECT NUMBER COUNT!

3 5 9 1

Alphabets

ABC Wonderland

Van

Use a pencil to trace the practice lines.

Trace the lines with your finger.

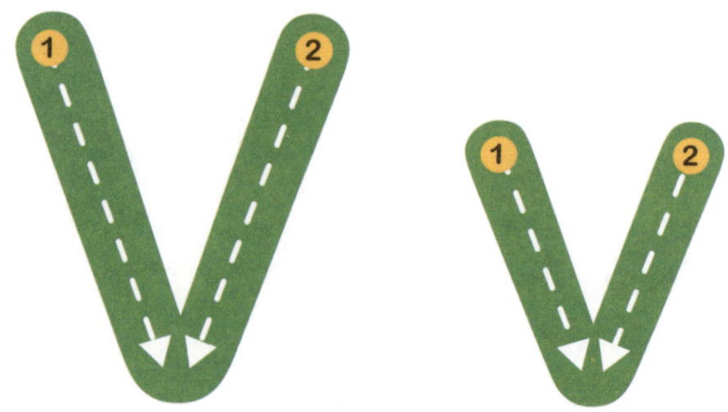

HOW MANY 'V' CAN YOU SPOT? CIRCLE THE CORRECT NUMBER COUNT!

(8) (4) (2) (3)

ABC Wonderland

Watermelon

Trace the lines with your finger.

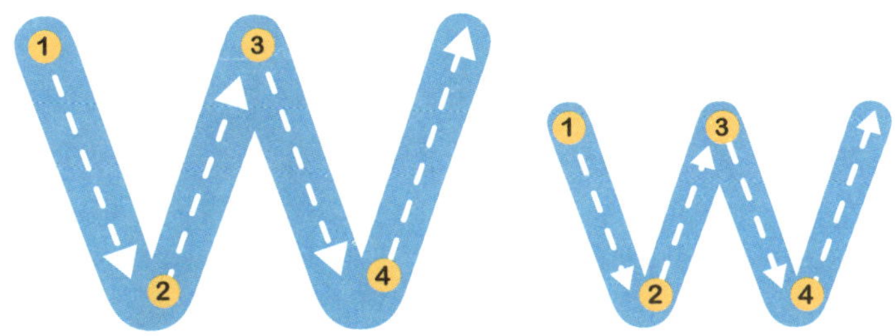

Use a pencil to trace the practice lines.

HOW MANY 'W' CAN YOU SPOT? CIRCLE THE CORRECT NUMBER COUNT!

2 5 9 4

Alphabets

ABC Wonderland

X-ray

Use a pencil to trace the practice lines.

Trace the lines with your finger.

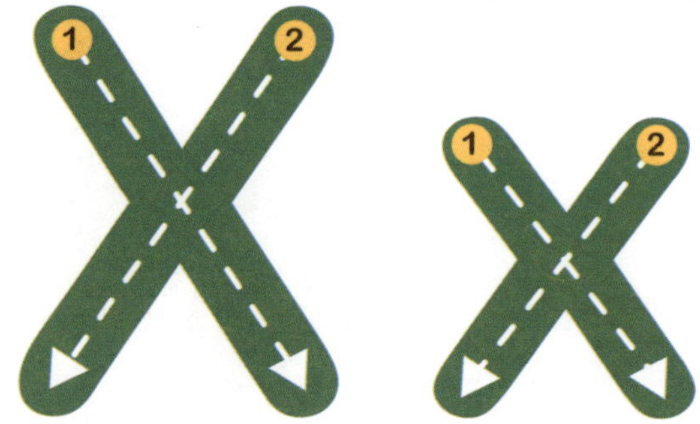

HOW MANY 'X' CAN YOU SPOT? CIRCLE THE CORRECT NUMBER COUNT!

(2) (4) (7) (5)

ABC Wonderland

Yawn

Trace the lines with your finger.

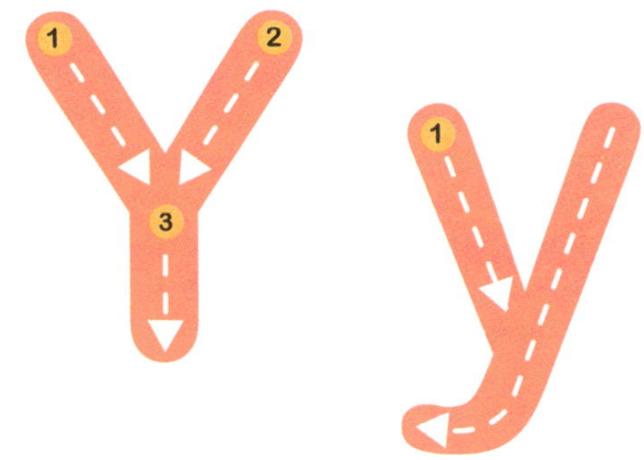

Use a pencil to trace the practice lines.

Y Y Y Y Y Y

y y y y y y y y

Y y Y y Y y Y y Y y

HOW MANY 'Y' CAN YOU SPOT? CIRCLE THE CORRECT NUMBER COUNT!

5 4 1 7

Alphabets

ABC Wonderland

Zoo

Use a pencil to trace the practice lines.

Trace the lines with your finger.

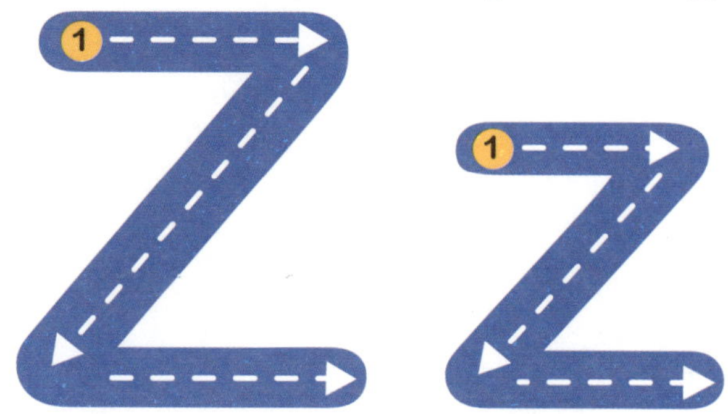

HOW MANY 'Z' CAN YOU SPOT? CIRCLE THE CORRECT NUMBER COUNT!

Types of Weather

Sunny

Cloudy

Rainy

Stormy

Snowy

Windy

Days of the Week

Sunday

Monday

Tuesday

Wednesday

Thursday

Friday

Saturday

Strengthening Little Hands for Writing!

Your child needs strong hand and finger muscles to control a pencil with ease. Check out these fun, hands-on activities that will help develop fine motor skills and improve their pencil grip—perfect for preparing little hands for writing!

Tear and Crumple

Tear up some soft tissue paper into small squares (about 1.5 to 2 inches). Ask your child to crumple the paper using the first three fingers of both their hands and roll them into tiny balls or scrunchies.

Roll and Shape

Give your child small pieces of dough or playdough. Ask them to roll the play dough into snakes using their palms and fingertips.

Pick and Sort

Hand your child a box of large, colourful beads and a pair of child-safe tweezers or tongs. Challenge them to pick up each bead with the tweezers or tongs and sort them by colour.

Squeeze and Release

Squeezing stress balls or soft smiley balls and releasing them is an excellent exercise for little hands. Alternatively, ask your child to squeeze their hands into a fist and then stretch out the fingers and wrists.

Spin and Control

Buy spinning tops with a slightly longer stem and ask your child to spin it using the first three fingers of their writing hand. Encourage the right-handed child to turn the top clockwise and the left-handed one to spin it in the anti-clockwise direction.

Peel and Stick

Give your child sheets of small stars or smiley stickers. Draw a straight line on a piece of paper and ask them to place the small stickers along the entire length.

Colour and Create

Draw or trace small squares and circles on a sheet of paper. Ask your child to colour them up using different coloured crayons or pencils.

Thread and Lace

Give your child large beads and a shoelace or thick string and ask them to thread the beads, which helps improve hand-eye coordination and finger strength.

Clip and Pinch

Hand out some clothespins (pegs) or binder clips and ask your child to clip them onto the edge of a box or piece of fabric.

Spray and Squeeze

Fill a small spray bottle with water and let your child spray plants or a chalkboard. The squeezing motion builds hand strength.

Drop and Aim

Give your child a coin or button and ask them to drop it into a narrow slot, like a piggy bank. This enhances finger control and coordination.

Stay Magical
Dreamer
SUPER!
GOOD
SUPER GOOD
FANTASTIC!!
AWESOME!
GOOD JOB!
NICE WORK!
NICE JOB
EXCELLENT!
WELL DONE!
SUPER GOOD
GOOD JOB
NICE JOB
GOOD JOB
EXCELLENT!
GOOD!
GOOD JOB
Cool Cool
Cool
HELLO
SUPER star
WOW!
SUPER star
Stay Magical
YOU'RE COOL